ENGINEERING FAITH

By

Sherica A. Matthews

Final edit by: Jennifer A. Jas

Cover by: KingRays

Book Consultation by Shalena D.I.V.A. Broaster

Engineering Faith

ISBN: 978-0-692-40367-9

Published by Beyond Barriers Publishing Company – a subsidiary of Live Life Beyond Barriers, LLC

ACKNOWLEDGEMENTS

To my parents, Dave and Shirley Matthews: I am so grateful that God chose you to be my parents. You are truly the reason that I am who I am today.

To Pastor Anthony Chatman: For seeing the greatness in me and for encouraging me to finally walk in my purpose.

To Toni Cheeks: For always being there for me during the good times and the not-so-good times. Thank you for your prayers, words of encouragement and your presence in my life.

To my godparents, Carvin and Sandra Brazelton: For taking me into your home and hearts with open love.

To my godsisters, Alex Brazelton and Cassidy Wheeler: For being my cheerleaders, motivators and confidants.

To my sister, Debra Matthews: For always being my biggest fan!

To my best and closest friends – Angela Holmes, Damita Mason, Sandra Affare, Tyaisha Blount, Kim Mason and Natasha Leon: Thank you for being there for me in the best and worst of times.

Last, but certainly not least, I want to thank God for choosing me to deliver this message. I thank God for allowing me to go through and GROW through the experiences that I have had that have shaped me into the woman I am today. I am so happy and grateful that God has aligned me with the right people and the right opportunities to make all of this possible.

TABLE OF CONTENTS

SECTION 1

INTRODUCTION

1 What is Engineering Faith?

What is engineering faith? Engineering faith is a term that I use to help reconcile the abstract world of spirituality with the more concrete, physical world. I chose to put these two words together because of what they mean individually.

> **Engineer** (verb) is defined: to create, plan, construct or manage.

> **Faith** is defined as: complete trust or confidence in someone or something; strong belief in God or in the doctrines of a religion.

When we put these two terms together, **Engineering Faith** means to create a plan or a formula to develop our trust and confidence in God.

I am an electrical engineer by degree and trade – I am hardwired to engineer: to create, plan and construct. I've worked in the oil and gas industry as an electrical engineer and project engineer for over 10 years. I was THAT kid in school. I was the one who LOVED math and science. Why? Because I love equations. I love figuring things out. I love finding solutions. And most solutions can be found using a mathematical equation.

Logic.

Science.

Reasoning.

That is the name of my game.

This served me very well all throughout my educational career. However, as I became an adult, I found it difficult to apply logic to every aspect of my life. In particular, it was difficult for me to define my spirituality because spirituality was such an abstract concept. Spirituality did not seem to follow logic, science or reasoning – let alone a mathematical equation. But I knew that spirituality fit into the equation of my life. I knew that I could not go on through life without acknowledging or developing my spiritual side. For a long time, I just couldn't figure out how to do it.

I was always told to:

> Just believe
>
> Just have faith
>
> Just try Jesus
>
> Just be like Jesus

That was my favorite one – Just be like Jesus – Um, last time I checked, Jesus was the Son of God. He was perfect. He was sinless. Last time I checked, I wasn't perfect, and I had sin in my life every day. HOW exactly was I supposed to be perfect like Jesus and live like Him and trust Him?

When I asked that question, I got all kinds of crazy looks. People actually looked at me as if I was speaking in another language. I was chastised for questioning God and questioning what I was being taught. I learned pretty quickly to be quiet and do the best that I could with what I had.

I developed a DIY mindset – I was going to "do it myself." Meaning that although I knew God existed, He was far away and didn't get involved in human life. And if I wanted anything done, I had to roll up my sleeves and do it myself. In my mind, I treated life as if it was a mathematical equation – whatever work I put in equated to the results I got out.

This mindset worked for me for a long time – up until adulthood, when life really started to happen. There were two significant life events that happened to me and shook up my world. My marriage was in trouble, and a close friendship I had invested a lot of time and energy into came to an abrupt end.

When I reached out for help and understanding from people in the Christian community during this time, I was told I should:

>Have bigger/stronger faith

>Just pray about it

>Remember that sometimes, bad things happen to good people

And my favorite – just be a martyr for God

So, yeah … none of that really resonated with me.

Have you ever heard that before? Perhaps you have felt that hopeless feeling when you're looking for concrete answers and the best anybody can tell you is, "Just have faith" or "Just believe God."

I felt hopeless because I thought that I did have faith. I thought that I did believe God. And look where that got me …

At least, that's how I felt in that moment.

After much struggle between what I thought I should do and what I was told I should do, I ended the marriage and spent the next year recovering and relearning who I was and who God was to me.

In hindsight, what was really happening was that I didn't know HOW to have faith. I didn't know HOW to apply faith in my life.

I knew how to apply logic and reasoning. But, as you may already know, things of the spirit don't always follow logic and reasoning. And me being the logical Type A person who loves plans, agendas and step-by-step guides – it did not work to apply the abstract concept of "Just have faith" to a very real and concrete problem. I could not just have faith or decide to believe without any questions, no way!

The biblical definition of real faith is found in Hebrews 11:1, "Faith is the substance of things hoped for, and the evidence of things not (yet) seen." My faith developed as a muscle does when you exercise: it began to grow and gain definition with each step I took. Your faith, too, will actually begin to set you apart from the rest – you will be different in all the right ways. When you start on your journey to engineering your faith into something tangible and concrete, you will find the answers you seek and the life you've always wanted.

2 PERSONALITY TYPES

There are four different personality types used in this book: the outcast, the people pleaser, the misfit/nonconformist and the logical thinker. I have personally experienced characteristics of all four of these personalities at some point in my life. It may not have been all four at the same time, but at least one or two at the same time. And if you're reading this, I'm sure you have, too. Breaking down the sections into four different personalities will help you to identify where you are in life and what areas of your inner self you need to work on. Don't get frustrated if one day, you find yourself being a people pleaser and the next day, you find yourself behaving like an outcast. This is normal. And don't think something is wrong with you because you can only identify with one personality type. This is normal, too. The point is that there isn't a specific mold that everyone fits into. You have to discover what your unique mold is and work within that.

To help you identify your mold and your personality, and also how to apply your faith, I have briefly defined each personality below.

What is an **outcast**?

- An outcast is a person who is rejected or cast out. I will tell you this – I know firsthand what it feels like to be an outcast.

- As I see it, being an outcast simply means that you explore your own faith, mind and style.
- You know who you are and what you stand for.
- You possess an authentic sense of yourself that makes you feel less pressure to be like everyone else.
- You can see around corners – you are able to observe what's going on around you, as if you were on the outside looking in.

What is a **people pleaser?**

- You want to make other people happy more than yourself – people pleasers will sacrifice their own happiness and their own well-being for the sake of others (especially women)
- Your primary goal is to be liked and appreciated in return by the people you try to please.
- A people pleaser has a hard time creating true relationships – you put on a façade, never allowing anyone to see or know the real you.

What is a **misfit / nonconformist**?

- A misfit is a person who doesn't always go with the flow or follow social norms.
- You may challenge the status quo by the way you think, the way you dress or the life decisions you choose to make.
- A nonconformist will usually take the less-beaten path. – You have the courage to do something different and unique.
- You define success by your own terms, and most people would not agree with you.

- You embrace your uniqueness – you stand out from the crowd! You know it is much more difficult to deny who you are than to accept yourself for who you truly are.
- You would rather take a risk and fail than live an inauthentic life.

What is a logical thinker? Of all the personality types we've discussed, this is my dominant personality type. One of the reasons that I enjoy math and science so much is because they are logical – there are formulas and proofs to prove results. I excel as an engineer because I love calculations. In my personal life, I love making plans and living from my calendar. I think and type in outlines and can visualize flowcharts. I love it when things are organized and in order. I feel completely lost and chaotic whenever my home or work environment gets out of order. I can't move forward until a logical order is restored.

- Logical thinkers can be reserved, as you analyze the world around you.
- You like to get to the bottom of things – curiosity is one of your strongest motives.
- You want to know what holds the world together deep down inside.

As you read each section, take note of which areas make you nod your head in agreement or which tips resonate with you. Go back and revisit those areas when you feel like you need a boost. If there is a section that doesn't seem to fit what you are going through at the time you read it, just know that the guide is here for you when the time is right and you need it.

3 How to Use This Book

This book is designed to be a reference guide as you are going through your day-to-day life. At any given moment, you could be experiencing one or more of the four different personality types.

I encourage you to read through this book all the way through at least once. You will find that it is a very easy read, packed with powerful information. I purposefully kept each section short. To me, the most valuable books are the ones that keep their messages clear and concise. Ultimately, I want this book to be a valuable resource for you. After you've read through it once, go back and reread the sections or chapters that really resonate with you. Keep this book with you for easy access and to use as a quick reference guide. You can flip to the section and chapter that most fits where you are at that time. You can use it as you move beyond theory to immediately apply it to your life.

In keeping with my commitment to my readers for clear and engaging content, I have also created a workbook that you can use in conjunction with Engineering Faith. The Engineering Faith Home Study offers you the opportunity to actively transform your life.

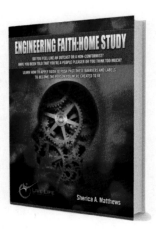

The activities, reflection questions and food for thought are designed to complement the tips in the book. Using both together will greatly enhance their effectiveness in your life. I'm excited about the journey ahead for you as you begin Engineering Faith ... let's get going!

SECTION 11

THE OUTCAST

4 CHOOSE TO BE POSITIVE

"Happiness is an attitude. We either make ourselves miserable, or happy and strong. The amount of work is the same." ~ **Francesca Reigler**

As an outcast, it is so easy to get mad at the world for making you feel like an outcast. It is also very easy to get mad at God for making you the way you are. You may also be mad at your parents for coming together to conceive you in the first place. As an outcast, it is so easy to find many reasons to be mad, angry and unhappy. The problem is that when you are mad, angry and unhappy, you will find the negative in everything and everyone. Finding the negative in every situation and in every person will only make you feel like even more of an outcast. Why? Because no one wants to be around a sourpuss! So your attitude will further drive you into the very place you don't want to be.

Anger and unhappiness touch every aspect of your life. When you feel angry and unhappy, you think negative thoughts. Those negative thoughts soon lead to negative actions. You may begin to speak harshly to people. You will put yourself in negative situations and environments. When you do that, you will begin to attract people who are just like you. Before you know it, you have created such a negative force around you that you will begin to feel hopeless about ever pulling yourself free from it. You may feel like an outcast, but that doesn't mean that you have a horrible life or that you are a horrible person. You are uniquely and wonderfully made in the image of God. There will be days when you can't find any other reason to be positive and smile, but dwell on this because it is the truth.

Choose to be positive. Choose to see the good in the people and situations around you. Choose to think positive thoughts and say kind words. When you choose to be positive, you will begin to attract people who like positivity. As you begin to attract people who are like you, you will begin to feel less and less like an outcast. When you choose to be positive, you choose to think positive thoughts. When you choose to think positive thoughts, you choose to act positively and you begin to feel positively. As you think good thoughts, you feel good and this positivity will begin to reflect itself in your actions. Soon, you will begin to create a life that you like instead of a life that you don't like or don't want.

Working as an engineer in the oil and gas industry, I find there is constant pressure to complete projects under budget, earlier than scheduled and with a higher quality than expected. While most seasoned professionals know that achieving all three goals is nearly impossible, it doesn't stop project managers and project directors from pushing their team members to the limit to accomplish all three objectives. As a result, the work environment is very negative. Many people are stressed, frustrated and angry. People tend to become mean and disrespectful, lashing out at one another out of frustration. It is almost expected that your personal relationships will suffer (many people are working on their second or third marriages as a result of bringing home their frustrations). Interestingly, most of the negativity begins with one person. In this supercharged and stressful environment, it only takes one person to create a never-ending negative cycle. One person says something negative to someone else, and they choose to take it to heart. That person in turn takes it out on someone else and before you know it, the negativity has spiraled out of control. It infects the workplace and then goes on to touch the lives of family and friends outside the office. Sadly, most people who are in this type of environment are aware that this is happening. Yet, they choose to stay there.

I have learned that I too can choose how I will respond to stress. I can be like everyone else and choose to be angry, choose to be frustrated and choose to be negative. Instead, I can choose to be positive and to look at the positive aspects of even the most negative situation. I have learned that while I cannot control what other people say and do, I can control what I say and do. So I choose to smile. I choose to be positive. And I choose NOT to take part in negative conversations. But don't get me wrong. I am human just like everyone else. That means that some days are better than others. But each day I wake up, I make the conscious decision to be positive and I strive to be intentional about maintaining positivity and happiness wherever I go.

You can't avoid negatives in life, so how can you offset any negative effect on your life and your attitude? Learning the power of positive thinking can help you stay positive even in the midst of life's most challenging circumstances. In your everyday life, you have a choice. You can choose to smile. You can choose to say a kind word to others and to yourself. Just as one small negative thought can turn into a giant ball of ugliness, a small positive thought can have the same power, blossoming into something beautiful.

The Message version of the Bible says:

Summing it all up, friends, I'd say you'll do best by filling your minds and meditating on things true, noble, reputable, authentic, compelling, gracious – the best, not the worst; the beautiful, not the ugly; things to praise, not things to curse ... Do that, and God, who makes everything work together, will work you into his most excellent harmonies.

5 Be Strong and Courageous

"Courage is what it takes to stand up and speak; courage is also what it takes to sit down and listen. ~ Winston Churchill

When you're feeling like an outcast, there will be times when you feel shy. You won't feel like your voice can be heard because you think no one sees you or you think people will criticize you and judge you. It is so important that you face these feelings directly; look your fears in the eyes. If you don't make yourself heard, no one will ever see you, hear you or take you seriously.

Part of the reason that you feel like an outcast is that you haven't found your path in life yet. You haven't found your place. You feel lost. You feel like an outsider. But you will never change the feeling of being an outsider if you don't find your voice and find your path. You can find your voice and your path by having faith in yourself and your journey. Trust your intuition and let it guide you in a direction that is more fulfilling than you could ever have imagined for yourself. Being courageous and strong can be really hard. But it can also be really amazing. When you do find your voice, you will find joy, passion and purpose. Best of all, you will feel the lightness that comes with speaking your truth.

Do you know the expression: closed mouths don't get fed? It means that if you don't open your mouth, you will not get what you need to survive. Ask for help. Ask for advice. Ask for guidance. Share your opinions.

When you step out and choose to be courageous, you will be surprised how many doors will open for you. But just because you choose to be courageous doesn't mean that you won't feel nervous or scared. You will. And just because you choose to be courageous doesn't mean that it will make things easier. It won't. Being strong and courageous makes things possible. It's scary, and requires you to push the limits of your comfort zone. It means you have to set and honor boundaries, make big and small changes and venture into the unknown at times. But you can do it!

Being strong and courageous will help you find your path and your purpose. Being strong and courageous may even cause you to make mistakes. But as a result, you will gain wisdom, you will become stronger. And most importantly, you will become more courageous because you will realize "Hey! I did it. I survived. And I became a better person in the process."

> *Being courageous will not make your journey easier, but it will make it possible. Possible for you to continue. Possible for you to overcome. Possible for you to find your breakthrough.*

As a young adult in college, I began to ask the difficult questions and challenge the status quo. While this was an exciting time for me to explore new directions, this also caused me to question and ultimately reject my family's religious beliefs. Because one of my college friends asked the question, "Have you received the Holy Spirit?" I began the journey of reading the Bible for myself. This journey led me to self-discovery and allowed me to discover God for myself. In doing so, I discovered that I did not share my friend's religious beliefs. But I also decided and gained the courage to say that I was not in agreement with the doctrine that I had grown up with and had been taught by my parents. That was not an easy decision to make. Nor was it an easy action step.

There I was, in my early 20s, standing up to and rejecting the very things that my parents held near and dear. It was absolutely scary. I wasn't sure how my parents would respond, but I knew that they wouldn't respond positively. I also knew that I would not have peace with myself if I didn't define my own beliefs and stand up for those beliefs. This took an extraordinary amount of strength and courage – something that I didn't even know I had until I was presented with this challenge. Through the internal work of self-motivating myself, I was able to stand up with confidence and declare my own beliefs. Digging deep to discover my own courage and strength stamped out any fear that I had. Finding my own courage and strength did not make my journey easier, it simply made my journey possible.

Take steps today, right now, to give voice to your thoughts and begin the journey on your chosen path. Get started by asking yourself the following questions:

- Where am I not speaking my truth right now?
- What am I afraid of if I do speak?
- What will happen if I choose not to speak?

Just as I learned, the spaces – the hard and scary ones – are the spaces that will become the building blocks of creating a life you will love. Finding your voice and speaking your truth will allow you to develop fulfilling relationships, find your purpose and live a life filled with joy.

> *For God has not given us a spirit of fear and timidity,*
> *but of power, love, and self-discipline.*
> ~ *2 Timothy 2:7*

6 LOVE EXACTLY WHO YOU ARE AND WHERE YOU ARE

*"You yourself, as much as anybody in the entire universe, deserve your love and affection." ~ **Buddha***

There will always be people who will judge you, make fun of you or even hate you. But if you love yourself and act like you love yourself, you will begin to attract more people who feel the same way about you as you do! You have to show the world that you are comfortable in your own skin. You have to show the world that you love you. And you love the journey that you are on. I'm sure you've heard the saying that you have to teach others how to treat you. So love yourself so others can learn how to love you too. Love where you are and be less critical of your journey. When you do, you'll find the blessing in the lesson. Everything that you go through has a purpose. But you'll miss it if you can't appreciate the way God created you and the journey that He allowed you to embark upon.

As you go throughout life, you will rock the boat. You will disagree with certain things and certain people. Part of being an outcast is that you don't fit in with the "norm." And when you don't fit because you have formed your own beliefs and your own way of being, there will be some people in life who will reject you. It could be your best friend. It could be your mother or father. But rejection will come. And it will hurt. But it is critical that during this time you love yourself more. It is during this time that you must remind yourself of how beautiful and wonderful God created you to be. So no matter what anyone says or how anyone treats you, nothing will change that fact. When you know this as fact, this will help you navigate the rocky road of being rejected or criticized.

When I questioned my family's religious beliefs, I made the decision to go against their firmly held convictions. This resulted in being rejected. As a result of being rejected, I felt as if I wasn't loved, that I was no longer good enough to be loved by my family. I couldn't understand how my family could treat me this way. I thought that if they loved me, even though I chose a different belief system, they would still accept me, or at least like me. But I had to learn to like myself and to love myself. Rejection has a way of making you question yourself – question who you are, question the decisions that you make, question where you are in life. But in the midst of questioning myself, there was still a sense of peace. A sense that I was right where I needed to be. Don't confuse having peace with being comfortable. You can have peace in an uncomfortable situation. Because I had peace, I was able to turn my focus to loving myself, loving who I am and loving where I am. And I also focused on the people who actually showed me love and acceptance. The more I loved myself, the more I was able to see and appreciate the love that was shown to me by God and others around me.

We all have great days where everything goes well: we feel good about the way we look, we say all the right things and we are getting things done! It's easy to love yourself on your good days. But the truth is you have to love yourself on the bad days too. When you're tired, anxious and have made a mistake (or two); that is when you need to love yourself the most. You are equally lovable at all times. God sees value in you and believes you are inherently worthy simply by being here.

So, how exactly do you love who you are and where you are? The best thing to do is simply show gratitude. Give thanks to God for making you just the way you are. Give thanks for the quirky way you smile, the way you walk, the way you talk and the way you think and reason. Give thanks for your sense of humor and your uncanny ability to bring peace to the room. Whatever characteristics make you uniquely you, give thanks for those. And then give thanks for your journey. Give thanks for your past experiences and the lessons learned. Give thanks for the upcoming experiences that will help you grow in wisdom and discernment. Give thanks for how everything is working out for your good to allow you to live the life you've always wanted.

Practice this as often as you can throughout the day. The first few times, you may find it difficult to be sincerely thankful for all the things that have made you an outcast. And your gratitude list may feel forced. But the more you say it, the more you will believe it, and the more you'll begin to truly love you for you.

When you learn to be thankful for who you are and where you are, it will show through your words and your actions and your attitude. You will look better, act better, and most importantly, you will feel better. A sense of unconditional self-love and acceptance will give you the foundation from which you can build a life that you have always dreamed of.

> *"Don't ever criticize yourself. Don't go around all day long thinking, 'I'm unattractive, I'm slow, I'm not as smart as my brother.' God wasn't having a bad day when he made you ... If you don't love yourself in the right way, you can't love your neighbor. You can't be as good as you are supposed to be." ~ Joel Osteen*

7 Continue to Think for Yourself

Information is Knowledge. Knowledge is Power.

Don't jump on the bandwagon of the status quo just to feel accepted. Sometimes, we become so desperate to fit in and to feel loved by people who push us away that we will change who we are, what we think and what we believe just to fit in. Don't do it! Resist the temptation. Instead, do just the opposite. Continue to think for yourself, no matter how different it is; no matter how against the grain it is. Be YOU! Continue to nurture your mental growth and your spiritual growth. If you decide to quiet your voice and allow others to think for you, and just accept what everyone says just to be accepted, they are not really accepting you. They are really accepting a fake you. In the end, you're still not getting what you want. What you want is for people to like you for you; to accept you for you.

In order to attract the right people into your circle, continue to do the things that will help you grow as a person. Gather as much information about a subject as possible before forming an opinion. Build your mental resources by reading, observing and listening. Then take time to reflect and evaluate. Listen to your elders as often as you can. Come up with your own conclusions and your own beliefs. If you take time to evaluate and judge based upon what you observe firsthand rather than what you've been led to believe, you are increasing your knowledge and thinking for yourself. When appropriate, share your thoughts with the right people. When you are confident in your own voice and when you are confident in forming your own beliefs, you will be able to stand your ground anytime anyone doesn't accept you for you. You will be able to let it roll off of your back and keep moving forward to the people who are supposed to be in your circle.

"Knowledge is power. Rather, knowledge is happiness, because to have knowledge – broad, deep knowledge – is to know true ends from false, and lofty things from low. To know the thoughts and deeds that have marked man's progress is to feel the great heartthrobs of humanity through the centuries; and if one does not feel in these pulsations a heavenward striving, one must indeed be deaf to the harmonies of life." ~ Helen Keller

Throughout my journey to define my own spirituality and to define who God is for myself, I continued to read the Bible, I started to do my own research and I began to ask the difficult questions. Especially in the settings of traditional church, this is usually not accepted. I was told on more than one occasion to "go home and ask my husband," even though it was clear at the time that I was not married or even close to being married. Despite the resistance, I continued to read, study, grow and learn. So when I did formalize my own spiritual beliefs, I could quickly and intelligently explain to others why I believe what I believe. This was not done to convince anyone to believe what I believe, but to simply answer the question whenever asked, or to defend my beliefs whenever I needed to. Because I had chosen to go against the status quo religious beliefs of my family, I had to be sure that "I know that I know that I know." (As my dad used to say.) Knowing why I believe what I believe increased my courage and confidence in declaring my beliefs. When I was able to verbalize my beliefs, I also gained the respect of most people. I was able to give clear, concise answers instead of a typical response of "Because ..." or "It's what I've always been taught" or my favorite, "Why don't you just try it and you tell me."

Because I am willing to learn and grow, I am also open to hearing opposing ideas. I have learned to live in harmony with those who do not share my same beliefs because I understand where they are coming from and I respect our differences. This step alone opens up new avenues to grow and learn.

Continue to gather information. Continue to learn. Choose what you want to believe in. Be confident in it. The more you learn, the more you grow and the more you can appreciate and respect the world and the people around you.

"To be yourself in a world that is constantly trying to make you something else is the greatest accomplishment." ~ Ralph Waldo Emerson

8 ACCEPT REJECTIONS AS BLESSINGS

"You could be the ripest, juiciest peach in the world, and there's still going to be somebody who hates peaches." ~ Dita Von Teese

This is one of the hardest lessons to learn – accepting rejections as blessings. Especially when the rejection causes the loss of a romantic relationship, a friendship or a family relationship. If we let truth be told, rejection SUCKS! And rejection HURTS! But we also know that there have been times in our lives when we have made poor decisions about whom we allow into our lives. We have perhaps trusted people who we shouldn't have trusted. We have listened to people whom we should not have taken advice from. We have loved someone who did not deserve our love and attention. We have even given someone one too many chances in our lives. Sometimes, God will intervene on our behalf in order to protect us from ourselves. And when He does intervene by removing someone from our lives or by NOT allowing someone to enter into our lives, we kick, scream, and cry out, asking God WHY? Instead of asking God WHY, ask God to lead you to the people who are supposed to be in your life. Ask God to lead you to people who will love you the way you need to be loved, respected and cared for.

"As I look back on my life, I realize that every time I thought I was being rejected from something good, I was actually being re-directed to something better." ~ Steve Maraboli

A few years ago, I lost two very important relationships to me: One was my fiancé; the other was one of my best girlfriends. My fiancé ended the relationship with no clear reason other than a vague, "It's not you, it's me." And one of my best girlfriends accused me of not being a good friend to her, although I was there for her during her fight with cancer less than six months earlier. Both of these relationships ended within months of each other. And they literally broke my heart in a million pieces. At that point in my life, I sometimes still struggled with accepting the fact that I was different from most people and I badly wanted to fit in and be accepted. The end of these relationships made me feel even more rejected than I normally felt and I could not understand why this was happening to me. I wondered what I had done to deserve this.

But once I stopped feeling sorry for myself and began to ask God to show me what I needed to learn from these relationships, I learned that these rejections were necessary. God was literally saving me from myself. If I had continued with the relationship with my fiancé, I would have ended up in another unhappy marriage. I was making too many compromises and giving too much without receiving what I needed in return. I had not yet learned the true meaning of a healthy relationship. As much as I hated to admit it, my ex did me a favor. The same is true for my friendship. I had made too many excuses and turned a blind eye too many times to bad behavior toward me. I did not ensure that there was balance in the relationship. She, too, did me a favor by ending the relationship because the relationship wasn't healthy for either of us. I have always been taught to believe that relationships take work. So I was willing to work on both relationships to do everything I could humanly do in order to make them work. In the end, neither of them would have worked out.

When you are able to accept rejections as blessings in disguise, you will begin to see that everything happens for a reason. Have faith that you may be spared from something worse or brought closer to something even better. At the very least, the experience will make you a stronger person and will teach you a lesson or two. And that is always a good thing! Stepping back and clearly looking at these relationships allowed me to define what I want in both my romantic relationships and what I want in a platonic friendship. And of course, I learned what I didn't want. I also learned and accepted my role in the demise of each of these relationships and started the inner work to correct my shortcomings. The loss of both of these relationships was painful, but it was one of the best things that could have happened to me. They not only taught me valuable lessons, but they also made room for me to receive the type of relationship I truly desired in my love life and in my friendships.

The next time you are confronted with an obstacle or hit a bump in the road only to later discover that it is a blessing, share it with others. Change how you think about missed opportunities, lost love or inconveniences and know that it is for the best … you just might not know it at the time.

9 Learn to Encourage Yourself

"When nobody else celebrates you, learn to celebrate yourself. When nobody else compliments you, then compliment yourself. It's not up to other people to keep you encouraged. It's up to you. Encouragement should come from the inside." ~ Joel Osteen.

Times are going to get rough every once in a while. People may not always be there to offer you an encouraging word. Even your closest friends may not be available when you need them or they may be going through their own storm just when you need them. Don't hold it against them personally. Having a support system is great but you can't be 100 percent dependent on others. When you can't get to your support system or your support system is unavailable, what can you do? What can you do when you are feeling discouraged? When you are feeling down and out? What can you do when you are feeling lonely and alone? When you just want to give up?

One thing that makes a difference is for you to take the time to encourage yourself along the way. You do this by reaffirming positive truths to yourself. You talk to yourself. Think of the person who you would normally talk to in this situation. What would that person say to you? Find a mirror, look yourself in the eye, and say to yourself what he/she would normally say to you. Speak life back into yourself. Speak an encouraging word to yourself. Remind yourself of how God broke the mold when he made you. Remind yourself that even though you feel alone, when you close your eyes and look within, God is still there. God will never leave you nor forsake you.

It took a lot of deprogramming, spending time with God and seeking answers in His word to learn how to speak life into myself, without having to count on others to keep me alive, spiritually ...

When I was going through my divorce, one of my favorite songs was "Encourage Yourself" by the Tri-City Singers. I literally had this song on repeat almost every day. This song resonated with me because I felt so alone in my marriage. My ex-husband had nothing positive to say to me or about me. The people who I thought would be there for me weren't there. They all thought that I was simply going through the first-year-marriage blues and didn't take me seriously. I felt so alone, as if I had to fight this battle on my own. Luckily, I did have a couple of people in my life who were there for me. But at some point, I felt that I was becoming a burden to them with my sob stories and crying. I felt that it simply wasn't fair to them for me to depend on them so much. This was my burden to bear, not theirs.

Even in the darkest times, I had to learn to encourage myself, to speak life back into myself. No one else is 100 percent responsible for me. I had to learn to be responsible for myself. So I learned to encourage myself through inspirational songs and thought-provoking quotes/readings. This, along with the few friends who were still there for me, helped me make it through a very difficult time in my life.

Learning to encourage ourselves is one of the vital things we must learn to do to keep our sanity and to stay on course. People come and go all the time. And the people who you are depending on may be going through a storm of their own and may not be able to be there for you like you want them to. But if you learn to encourage yourself when you are alone, and you have healthy relationships with others who can encourage you when they can, you can make it through just about anything.

The next time you need a spark of encouragement, say one of these affirmations to yourself:

- I am working hard to overcome obstacles and find my path
- When I panic, this means I am learning
- I will be okay
- I will do my best; my best is good enough
- I will not always be suffering like I am right now. Someday, I will look back at this time and see the lessons I have learned
- I am learning more and more every day
- It's okay to have good days and bad days
- I will overcome this!
- God is with me, always

There are times when you find it is easier to encourage others rather than say these words to yourself. And that's okay! By encouraging others, especially those who may be going through similar struggles, you are really encouraging yourself. You end up helping yourself without even realizing it but you will feel the positive effects of those words and actions.

10 SPEND TIME ALONE WITH GOD

We are more than just physical beings. We are spiritual beings as well. And if we don't take the time to nurture our spiritual selves with prayer, meditation and reading religious/spiritual texts, we will never feel complete or secure. We will never know who God created us to be or what we should do with our lives. All of the answers that we seek about life are within our spirit and the Spirit of God. The answers are not in our circumstances. The answers are not in our family and friends. All of our answers are in God.

> *You are more than. . .*
> > *Your past*
> > *Your financial situation*
> > *Your job*
> > *Your personality*
> > *Your triumphs*
> > *Your failures*
> *You are a child of God ~ **John 1:12***

Knowing who you are, loving who you are and embracing who you are extends past the physical – it includes the spiritual. You have to know and love your whole self (physically and mentally) in order to live life fully. Denying any part of yourself is still denying yourself.

My spiritual journey is a continuous one. It truly started with one simple question by a friend so many years ago. And it continues today. The journey to discovering and defining who God is to me has led me to discover who I truly am spiritually. And this has made it easier for me to accept who I am in this world. Embracing both sides helps me to be more confident about who I am, in spite of difficulties, circumstances and adversities.

I invite you to do the same. Your spiritual journey is a highly personal journey. Whether you're Christian, Jewish, Muslim, Hindu or Buddhist, you must define for yourself who God is and who you are in God. God desires "alone time" with us. He wants a personal relationship with you. When you know this and are confident in this, you can then align your spiritual self with your physical self. This starts the physical self-discovery journey where you learn who you really are, what you were created for and your purpose for this moment in time. My journey followed this path and continues to follow this path. I spend time on a regular basis in rediscovery/remembering who I am in God. The learning never stops and the revelations never stop unless you do.

Spending time alone with God can provide the best nourishment for your body and soul. Without time alone with God, you may find needs unmet and you will never truly know the abundant life He gives. Spending time alone with God rids our minds of distraction so that we can focus on Him and hear His Word. By abiding in Him, you will be able to enjoy the personal relationship He so desires with you, and you will come to truly know Him and His purpose for your life.

> *"The time you spend alone with God will transform your character and increase your devotion. Then your integrity and godly behavior in an unbelieving world will make others long to know the Lord."* ~ ***Charles Stanley***

11 EMBRACE YOUR PERSONALITY (UNIQUENESS) TO FIND YOUR PURPOSE

"Choosing authenticity means nurturing the connection and sense of belonging that can only happen when we let go of what we are supposed to be and embrace who we are." ~ Brené Brown, Ph.D.

Be authentically you. God created you just the way He did for a purpose. If you reject the way He created you, then you'll never find your path or your purpose in life. You cannot embark on the journey that was uniquely created for you if you cannot love and accept the unique way God created you so that you CAN go on this journey. When you try to be someone you are not, or you try to fit in by belittling or downplaying certain aspects of yourself, then you will not be equipped for the path that you are to take. This can make you feel lost and confused. When you embrace your personality and the way God made you, you may feel uncomfortable for a minute, but you will find the freedom that only comes from knowing your purpose and that freedom lasts a lifetime.

"Freedom is being who you are unapologetically." ~ **Dr. Robin Smith**

Learning to love and accept who you are is a journey. But once you begin your journey, you will discover how the very things that set you apart are the very things that will aid in your success. It could be anything from your looks to your personality; loving every part of you will attract others who love that same quality, or it will offer opportunities to those who need your qualities. The next thing you know, you'll be on your road to success.

I began journaling at a young age. It was my form of self-therapy because I felt that no one understood me and no one cared what I really thought. So I would write everything down to get it off my chest. And once I wrote it down, I found it easier to dissect how I felt and come up with solutions. During one of the most trying times of my life, my divorce, I wrote A LOT! When I sought help for my marital problems, in an effort to not have to repeat myself, I would copy and paste my journal entries to my pastor, counselor or friends. Everyone was so amazed at my level of written communication – my attention to detail, my thought process that was captured on paper, my ability to capture both emotions and logic in writing. These were the very qualities that I tried so long to hide and suppress (especially outside of the workplace). For the first time, someone actually found value in it. But it wasn't enough for someone else to find value in the gifts I have. I had to find value and appreciate it for myself. And that didn't happen until years later. A very good friend and pastor of mine urged me for years to share my story. One day, I took the time to re-read all of my journal entries. It was in that moment that I found value in my gifts. I rediscovered who I was and fell in love with me – all of me – the good, the flaws, the logical thinking, the girl who didn't quite fit in, the girl who had a lot to say but kept most of her opinions to herself … I saw her, I heard her and I fell in love with her.

With continued prayer and meditation, I fell in love with myself. I finally discovered who I really was and how to use my uniqueness to accomplish a bigger goal. When I did, I realized one of my purposes in life. It is to help other people who are just like me. It is to help people through my speaking and writing to overcome their own fears and obstacles that have been holding them back. It is to share my wisdom and knowledge with others. It is to say to you all of the things that I wish someone had said to me to help make my journey through life better. That is one of my purposes in life. It took me years to get here. But when I got here, doors began to open for me left, right and center. People and opportunities were lined up in my path to lead me and guide me to my life's work. And here I am working with you. If I hadn't accepted all of who I am, those same people and opportunities may have presented themselves, but the outcomes would not have been the same. I probably would have missed them altogether or I could have recognized them but not known what to do with them. The sooner you fully love, accept and embrace who you are, the sooner you'll discover your purpose and how to use your uniqueness for your purpose.

When you find yourself wondering how to embrace what makes you YOU, spend some time in prayer and quiet reflection. Think back to your childhood and remember those dreams you had of what you wanted to do with your life. Reflect on those things that brought you joy and ignited a passion deep inside of you. Have an honest conversation with God; talk to Him about what you're thinking about. Listen for His voice within your heart. Be open to what He is saying both through his Word and also through the people or experiences He brings into your life.

You may also do what I do and write it all down. Writing it down not only gives you an opportunity to share your thoughts and feelings, it also offers you a chance to review your reflections.

When you can look back at your thoughts, you will begin to see the hidden details. God will reveal His purpose in all of those pieces of the puzzle. Be committed to finding out who you are and embrace yourself and your dreams.

REFLECTION

Use the lines below to express your thoughts and insights gained in this section. Describe how you can apply what you've learned in your everyday life.

_____

_____

_____

_____

_____

_____

_____

_____

_____

_____

_____

_____

_____

_____

_____

_____

SECTION III

THE PEOPLE PLEASER

12 PLEASE YOURSELF FIRST

*"It's not selfish to love yourself, take care of yourself,
and to make your happiness a priority. It's necessary."*
~ Mandy Hale

How can you make other people happy if you can't even make yourself happy? Too many times, we pour our time and energy into others and do all the things to make other people happy. But in the end, we are not happy. Now, I know that you are a genuinely good person. And you happily give and serve others. And it does give you a sense of fulfillment when you know you've done something to make someone else happy. So, you go around looking for ways to give to others and put a smile on everyone else's face.

But who makes you happy? Do you know what makes you happy? Do you know how to make yourself happy?

It is important to know how to make yourself happy because you are teaching the world how to give and pour back into you. If you are in a constant mode of pouring into others, and you don't pour back into yourself, your tank will run dry.

And it is important that you take care of yourself first. Not last.

Not somewhere in between. First. You must take care of yourself first so that you are at your BEST in all that you do. Take care of your mind. Take care of your body. Take care of your spirit. It may sound upside down, but when you put your needs at the top of the list it actually helps you to be more present for other people. In this way, I'm much more likely to respond to their needs effectively instead of reacting in a way that makes things worse.

In the end, people will judge you anyway. Don't live your life impressing others. Live your life impressing yourself.

Growing up, I was taught that I had to belong to a certain church and a certain religion in order to achieve salvation and eternal life after death. Anyone who did not belong to this church had no chance at salvation. However, even if I was a part of this church, there was no assurance that I would achieve salvation, either. Even to my young mind, this simply did not make sense to me. It did not make sense that God would make it so hard and almost impossible to achieve an afterlife in heaven. It did not make sense that God would exclude millions of people around the world who were not members of this church from achieving salvation (especially since the only records of this church exist in the United States). Because this didn't make sense, I chose not to become a Christian at that time. This was a really tough decision because I always strived to make my parents happy in everything I did. I wanted to make them proud. Making the decision to choose a different spiritual path came with its consequences.

It seems that no matter how hard I worked, no matter how many straight A report cards I brought home, no matter how good a daughter/sister I was, no matter how good a person I tried to be: it was never good enough. I just couldn't live up to everyone's expectations. At first, this bothered me on a deep level because I knew that I disappointed my parents. I knew that I broke their hearts with my decision. While most people I knew chose to stay on the path on which they were raised, I couldn't do that. I tried to return to the teaching from my childhood, but it just didn't sit well with me. I couldn't pretend to agree and believe in something I did not believe in, just to make my parents happy. I had to sleep with my conscience every night. And my conscience would not let me live a lie.

Making the decision to choose a different spiritual path was difficult. But I am happy that I did. Choosing a different spiritual path has taught me numerous lessons in love, forgiveness and patience. It has taught me that I have insurmountable courage and strength within me. And it has allowed me to seek God for myself and to know God for myself. If I had not made a decision to make myself happy and to do what was best for me, I would have missed all of these learning and growing opportunities.

I found the key to greater happiness is embracing my needs before others and putting myself first. You want to get on the path to loving yourself. Believe in your own ability to create, comfort and love. Do what you need to feel alive, vibrant and healthy in the most positive of ways. Do things for yourself that feel good – things that don't produce any negative feelings of remorse, anger or shame. I have found that when you feel good, you radiate goodness. It's infectious – everyone else wants to be around you, including you!

13 Don't be so Hard on Yourself

"I will hold myself to a standard of grace, not perfection." ~ Emily Ley

Allow yourself to make mistakes. This is how you grow and learn, especially if you know that you have done the work and have done the absolute best you can. In hindsight, there will always be things you can do differently. But remember to treat yourself how you want others to treat you: forgive yourself and show yourself grace and mercy.

Love is the antidote when you find yourself being too hard on you. Learn how to love yourself. Love is patient. Love is kind. Love doesn't keep account of wrongdoing. Criticizing everything that you do, judging yourself and comparing yourself to others is NOT loving yourself.

Choosing to treat yourself with grace adds strength to your person. When you love yourself and are kind to yourself, you will begin to feel good about yourself. Your self-confidence will be improved and you will be more courageous.

Being too hard on yourself doesn't make you feel any better. It makes you feel less than, down-and-out, unworthy. When you are in this negative state of mind, you will begin to attract more negative things. You won't feel good. Your self-esteem will suffer. Your self-confidence will suffer.

Beating yourself up because you aren't perfect doesn't solve anything. But picking yourself up and learning from your mistakes will solve future struggles.

You aren't this hard on your friends. Or even your enemies. So why are you this hard on yourself? Let it go.

I will never forget when I was a junior/senior in college – which tends to be the hardest year in the electrical engineering curriculum. All through college, I made nothing less than a B in all of my classes. But this semester, I really struggled in one particular class. No matter how much I studied, no matter how many times I went to the professor or teacher's aid for help, I just wasn't getting the subject matter. But I never gave up ... until the end of the semester. A week before final exams, I realized that there was no hope for me passing this class. This was a tough pill for me to swallow. I immediately felt a sense of shame and failure. Self-defeating thoughts began to run through my head such as:

"You're not cut out to be an engineer."

"You're not as smart as you think you are."

"Your best isn't good enough."

And because I spent so much time and energy studying for that one class, my grades in my remaining classes began to fall. So one week before finals, I had to make a decision. I had to choose between:

A. Giving it the old "college try" and putting everything I had into passing the final exam in hopes of getting a D which my professor would help me bump up to a C. In the meantime, the best I could hope to make in my other classes was a semester grade of a C.

B. Let go of this one class and put all of my concentration into my remaining four classes. I could still manage to have a B average in my other classes, but I would fail this one class and bear the embarrassment of having to retake the class.

After much contemplating, crying and a sleepless night or two, I went with option B.

And, as it turned out, it wasn't so bad. I did fail that one class. But I made a B in each of my other classes. AND my overall GPA was still above a 3.5 (which is an amazing feat in and of itself). No one judged me. No one criticized me. I wasn't kicked out of the engineering program. And I wasn't looked down upon. None of the fears that I had came true. As a matter of fact, when I re-took the class the following semester, I passed it with flying colors.

If I had stayed in a place of being hard on myself, beating myself up and not allowing myself to make mistakes, I would not have had an overall successful semester. If I had listened to all the fears and lies that my ego told me, I would never have become an engineer.

The next time you find you are being hard on yourself because you made a mistake, try to take a step back from the situation. Instead of focusing on the negatives, ask yourself what good things came out of the circumstance. You'll be amazed at the variety of answers! It could be that you've learned something new about yourself, or you've grown in a way you wouldn't have if you hadn't gone through the situation. At the very least you will have a better idea of how to handle similar situations in the future and you'll have gained a new skill or two.

14 ALLOW GOD TO TAKE CARE OF THE WORLD

"Incredible change happens in your life when you decide to take control of what you do have power over instead of craving control over what you don't." ~ Steve Maraboli

No human being can carry the weight of the world on her shoulders. Attempting to do so will only decrease the quality of your life and shorten your life. Your life is much more valuable and God has bigger plans to use you to impact the world. But, you must first let go. Relax. Let Go.

Instead of being so concerned with taking care of the world – running here and there to fill everyone's needs and requests – stop and recognize that you are not God. You are not responsible for EVERYONE's well-being. You are not responsible for others' decisions and actions. You are not responsible for carrying the weight of the world on your shoulders.

When you try to take care of the world instead of letting God do it, you get completely worn out. You won't have the energy or strength to carry on for a long period of time. Why? As a human being, you weren't designed to be in charge of everything. And because you weren't designed to carry the weight of the world, you will inevitably fail at a job that you weren't qualified to do in the first place. You won't be able to satisfy everyone. You won't be able to please everyone. You can't expect a stallion, not matter how strong he is, to carry the weight of an elephant.

But when you decide to let go of the weight of the world, and turn all of your concerns and struggle to God, an AMAZING thing happens. You become happier. You become healthier. You become a better version of you. And that's all anyone really wants.

> Allow yourself to be free.
> Allow yourself to let go.
> Trust God.
> Believe that God has your best interest at heart and will work everything out for your good.

> *And we know that God causes everything to work together for the good of those who love God and are called according to His purpose for them.* ~ **Romans 8:28**

I remember that feeling of never being good enough: it didn't matter how many As I got in school, how attentive I was as a daughter/sister/friend or how hard I tried to be a good Christian. It just seemed like nothing I did was good enough. I just couldn't seem to live up to everyone's expectations. I carried around this burden: that I must be a representative of my family, of the Christian community, a role model for my siblings, an example student at school, and the list goes on and on. I felt so overwhelmed at times. It was hard keeping up with all the responsibilities that I placed on myself. As a result, it came to a point where I wasn't enjoying life. I wasn't having fun. I was too busy trying to be everything to everybody. I had to learn that this was not my burden to bear. I felt responsible for the world. I felt that any failure on my part was catastrophic to the world (worst outcome) or that I would be an utter letdown to my family and community (best outcome). But this is not my burden to bear, nor is it your burden. When God created us, He created us with the power to choose. Along with that power to choose comes the possibility of making mistakes. God knew this. That is why He has offered us forgiveness and promises not to hold our mistakes against us. Because we are imperfect, He did not give us the weight of the world to bear. That is His job. So why would I want to take that from Him? I have enough to keep me busy just living, learning, growing and handling my own life, let alone the weight of the world.

> "You must learn to let go. Release the stress. You were never in control anyway." ~ *Steve Maraboli*

Learning how to "Let go and let God" comes down to this: letting go of your own will. Submitting to God's will and letting Him lead will bring you joy and peace, even during difficult times. When you let God do what He is good at, it frees you up to be the best you YOU can be!

15 ALWAYS BE TRUE TO YOURSELF

Always be true to yourself. Don't change your wants, desires, beliefs or goals just to make other people happy or to be accepted.

> *"Always be true to yourself. Never try to hide who you are. The only shame is to have shame. Always stand up for what you believe in. Always question what other people tell you. Never regret the past ... it's a waste of time. There's a reason for everything, every mistake, every moment of weakness, every terrible thing that has happened to you. Grow from it. The only way you can ever get the respect of others is when you show them that you respect yourself. And most importantly, do your thing and never apologize for being you."* ~ **Unknown**

I know about this all too well. When you are focused on pleasing other people and being accepted by others, you will begin to lose sight of yourself and who you are. You begin to compromise your values, desires, wants or needs just to make someone else happy or to gain someone else's approval. But what you don't realize is that in the end, the people you were trying to please or gain acceptance from won't know the real you. They will only know or like the façade of the person who you portrayed yourself to be –

not the person you were created to be. The truth will always eventually come out and you will do more harm than good. You will lose the friendships that you thought you had, you will feel embarrassed and you will lose respect from those around you.

Instead, when you choose to be yourself at all times, you will attract and gain the attention of people who value you for you. And when you surround yourself with people who actually value the real you, they will want to serve you as much as you want to serve them. The relationship will be much more balanced. As you give to others by operating as the person God created you to be, others will give back to you. You will feel more fulfilled, happy and at peace.

> *He grants a treasure of common sense to the honest. He is a shield to those who walk with integrity.* ~ **Proverbs 2:7**

As you may know, I have been married before. One of the reasons why the marriage ended was because my spouse was not truthful about who he truly was. He wasn't honest about his jobs, his finances, his childhood, his home, etc. He wasn't honest about who he was, where he came from, and how he became the person he is today because he had masterfully created an alternate persona that he wanted ... needed ... the rest of the world to believe about him. When confronted with the truth, he desperately held on to this alternate persona in a frantic attempt to maintain his image: in front of me, his friends and those around him. This was extremely painful to me because the things he was not truthful about, if he had been honest about them in the very beginning, would not have been deal- breakers for the relationship. Because he lied to me, because he hid the truth of who he really was, I realized that I did not fall in love with him. I fell in love with someone he made up. And because he refused to admit the truth, even when presented with tangible evidence, the relationship ended.

Changing who you are, twisting the truth about what you believe, what you want or what you desire will never end well. Especially in romantic relationships, men and women alike have a tendency to compromise what they want or need in the relationship for the sake of keeping the relationship alive. What many of us fail to realize is that when we do that, we are ultimately damaging the relationship. Hiding the truth, compromising the basic premises of who we are and what we need are like cracks in the foundation. With the pressures of time and the mounting weight of maintaining these untruths, the cracks will spread, and eventually the foundation will fail. Everything that you worked so hard to keep will fall to pieces. In the end, it is not worth it.

Remember that any time you compromise the story of YOU, you are actually compromising your integrity. When you are true to yourself, wonderful things begin to happen:

- You feel good, in a simple and vibrant way
- Your nagging inner voice is finally quiet
- You feel comfortable in your own skin
- It's easier to manage your life – no need to keep track of any lies or charades
- When you're not trying to impress anyone, your muscles relax and you can breathe
- You find it's easier to focus, you're less distracted
- You begin to make decisions confidently, without always second-guessing yourself

When you are true to yourself, you gain a sense of empowerment. You no longer have to look for love and acceptance outside of yourself because you give that to yourself. You now have the freedom to be whoever you want to be and be loved for it. This self-worth is then reflected back to you with relationships that accept and support you.

16 SET BOUNDARIES

Let's be clear: setting boundaries will not increase the number of friends in your life or make you the most popular person. But establishing healthy boundaries will help eliminate people who do not belong in your life, and make it clear to you the people who do belong in your life.

> *"The first thing you need to learn is that the person who is angry at you for setting boundaries is the one with the problem."* ~ **Drs. Cloud and Townsend**

When you begin to authentically be yourself, there will be some people who won't like it. They want you to conform to their ways of being, thinking and acting. Some will even try to pressure you into being who they want you to be, doing what they want you to do. This is why boundaries are important. Think of boundaries as a line drawn on the ground with paint. You can set your boundary as close to you or as far away from you as you'd like. The purpose of boundaries is to ensure that everyone maintains a boundary of respect. Some people have personal space boundaries where they do not like people to be within so many inches of their face. Some people have verbal boundaries where they do not like for people to use profanity in their presence. Others have boundaries related to money, sex, types of conversations or even types of dress. Boundaries will be different for every person. And just because one thing may be okay for Johnny doesn't mean that it has to be okay for you. Set your boundaries with people so that you feel comfortable and safe without imposing on someone else's boundaries.

When you do not know your own boundaries or have not communicated your boundaries, you will find yourself in situations where you feel used, taken advantage of or disrespected. When you feel this way, and these feelings are consistent, it could lead to the dissolution of the relationship, whether it is friendship, romantic or professional.

> *Setting boundaries is a way of caring for myself. It doesn't make me mean, selfish or uncaring because I don't do things your way. I care about me, too.*

I'll never forget having a "heated discussion" with a family member regarding my personal preference for religious worship several years ago. At the time, most people in my family knew that I had chosen to deviate from the religious choice of my upbringing. I'd been affiliated with a different church for at least five years at this point. But certain family members still had not accepted this as true and would often chastise me for turning my back on "the truth." During one of these discussions, this particular family member became very irate with me and began raising her voice at me. I calmly told her that we are both adults. We can express a difference of opinions in a respectful manner. If I can respect you by not raising my voice at you, I expect the same in return. Well, this further irritated my family member and she told me that because of who she was, she could talk to me any way she wanted to because she was right and I was wrong. So I replied that if she could not speak to me in a respectful manner, then I would end the conversation by hanging up the phone. I explained that this is not me trying to be rude. But rather this was my way of removing myself from a situation that I felt was disrespectful to me. Well unfortunately, I had to hang up the phone because this family member continued down the path of being disrespectful to me. At the time, it hurt that I had to enforce my boundaries. But I was at peace with it because 1) I had clearly communicated to her what my boundaries were, and 2) I had communicated to her what would happen if she continued to cross those boundaries.

One thing that I want to point out is that at no point in time did I try to force her to respect me. You cannot control the actions of another person. The only person that you have control over is yourself. So in this situation, I took control of myself. I did not lose my temper. I did not disrespect her in return. I simply removed myself from the situation because I was the only person in that situation that I could control.

Was this family member upset with me by how I handled the situation? Yes, she was. We did not speak for a week or two. But the next time we had a conversation and I expressed to her that I was feeling disrespected, either the conversation topic changed or she changed her voice/attitude so that she would not cross my boundaries. Now, we have mutual respect for each other.

> *"You teach people how to treat you by what you allow, what you stop, and what you reinforce."* ~ **Tony Gaskins**

A great way to set boundaries is to make a list of what you will never tolerate in your life. Write down those things that have bothered you in the past – be sure to include aspects of every part of your life (home, work, relationships, spiritual path, etc.).

Now make a list of how you would you like to strengthen your boundaries in the various areas of your life. For example, write down "I want to strengthen my boundaries around ____ by _____. Next, decide what kind of boundary you need to establish in order to stop the unwanted behavior and then figure out how you will deal with it. If someone has a strong reaction to a boundary you have set, remain calm. A calm and friendly tone will help you when you communicate your needs. Setting boundaries lets people know that you respect yourself. Boundaries are empowering – just imagine how good you will feel when you begin drawing the line more often and reap the rewards of self-respect.

17 KNOW WHO REALLY LOVES YOU

I asked God to protect me from my enemies, then I started losing "friends."

Realize that some people you are trying to please do not always have the best intentions for you.

Sometimes, it can be hard to tell the difference between your real friends and your fake friends. We live in a society where we have all gotten so good at hiding our real selves. We hide behind our work, our family, and we even hide behind our social media profiles. On social media, we can be anybody we want to be. We create the picture of ourselves that we want the world to see. Although you have decided to live life authentically and be your true self, it doesn't mean that other people will do the same, and it doesn't mean that other people will value the real you.

Be with people who know your worth. You don't need too many people to be happy. Just a few real friends who appreciate you for who you are.

I learned this lesson the hard way. I was friends with a young lady for almost three years. I was so thankful for her because she showed up in my life when I needed a friend the most. Yes, she was different than most people I typically hung out with. But her differences were nothing that I thought would make me compromise who I was. There were times when she would say things to me that were really harsh or simply uncalled for. I would make up excuses for her, saying to myself, "Well, that's just how she is!" This was just how she was raised. She told me all about her childhood: the rough neighborhood she grew up in and how she used to be teased mercilessly. As a result, she learned to be very tough and brash as a way of protecting herself. Unfortunately, it was usually at the expense of others.

Shortly after my fiancé and I broke up, she and I took a trip together. The breakup was fresh in my mind and I really needed a friend. Well, as soon as we arrived at our destination, she told me that she and her then-boyfriend didn't think that I was being a good friend. They thought that I could have been doing more to plan double dates with them (when I was engaged) and even after we broke up, I should not have asked to come over to their house because it was not something that I normally do. (On this particular occasion, I had been feeling very emotional and didn't want to go straight home after work. I called and asked if I could come over and I was told yes. Yes, I didn't typically come over in the middle of the week. But I just needed a friend and a shoulder to cry on). Words were exchanged and in the end, I realized that our friendship had been one-sided for a long time. I just didn't recognize it because I was too busy making excuses for her. When our friendship ended, I was heartbroken because it was so close to the ending of my engagement. And I couldn't understand why God was allowing this to happen. But once I began the healing process and began to see her for who she really was, I realized that she was in my life for a reason and only for a short season. She was not meant to stay in my life forever. We were not a good fit for each other in a friendship. And that is okay. When I decided to let the friendship go, I felt more at peace and I created room for other genuine people to enter into my life. Whether these people are in my life for a season or for a lifetime ... only time will tell.

Take inventory of the people you live with, work with and play with. Do their words match their actions? Are you constantly giving to someone and then not receiving anything back? Are they constantly putting you down or saying something critical? Do they lift you up?

Knowing who loves you and who is truly a friend versus those who aren't can save you a lifetime of heartache.

> *Stop doing things for some people if you find that they're starting to expect it from you rather than appreciating it.*

When people love you, they will work to heal your old wounds and try to protect you from new wounds. They will accept you at your worst, all the while helping you to achieve your best. When people really love you, they won't try to change you but they also won't let you settle for anything less than what God created you to be. They'll believe in you even during those times when you don't quite believe in yourself.

And they will never give up on you. God displays His love for us in all of these ways and calls us to do the same for each other.

18 Know Your Worth

Know your worth. All relationships are about give and take. Know your worth enough to walk away from relationships that do not serve you as much as you serve your partner.

Know your worth. Know the difference between what you're getting and what you deserve.

Knowing your worth is something that many of us have to be reminded of every day. Myself included. Both my godmother and my godsister gave this piece of advice to me. But it took me years to really come to understand what it means to know your worth. I often confused knowing my worth with being arrogant or self-centered. Knowing your worth is really having confidence in who God created you to be. Knowing that every single aspect of you has a special meaning and a special purpose. Whoever you choose to share yourself with will greatly benefit from your presence in their lives simply because of who you are and who you were created to be. When you know your worth, and when you know the worth of those around you, you create more balanced relationships. You create relationships where there is an equal amount of giving and taking. You create relationships where all involved feel loved and appreciated for who they are, who they were created to be and what they bring to the table.

When you find yourself in a relationship where you do not feel this way – you do not feel love and appreciation and there is not balance, then you must remove yourself from that relationship. As hard as it may seem, it is necessary. When you stay in relationships that are unbalanced and you do not feel loved and appreciated, you will begin to feel drained and used, you will question yourself and your abilities, and you won't feel good about yourself. But when you are in relationships that are balanced and you feel loved and appreciated, you will also begin to feel empowered to take on the world. You know that you have the love and support to be, do and conquer anything that comes your way.

The following story is for mature audiences only

A couple of years ago, I was set up on a blind date by a dear friend of mine. My date was a young man who was handsome, had a career and was pursuing his MBA degree. We agreed to go out to dinner after a presentation he made for his MBA program. Dinner went well. I enjoyed the conversation ... until the end of the evening. With a straight face, he said, "You and I are both adults. I'm attracted to you and you're attracted to me. Why don't we go ahead and have sex?" In that instance, I felt a mix of emotions. I was shocked, angry, appalled and disgusted. After a couple of hours with me, he wanted me to share an intimate experience with him such as sex. I don't even think he knew my last name. But he wanted me to share my body with him. He didn't know how intelligent I was. He didn't know what drives me or motivates me. He didn't know anything about me. But he wanted me to give him one of my most precious gifts. I did not feel valued at all. I did not feel that he knew me or even wanted to get to know me. He didn't want to know what makes me happy or what makes me sad. He didn't want to know what he could do to serve me in my life and what I could do to serve him in his life.

Needless to say, the date ended shortly after that. As he was walking me to my car (despite my protest), he made the comment that I would regret this decision in the morning. Talk about adding insult to injury! He clearly did not know who Sherica Matthews was, and he clearly did not know my worth. I turned to him, looked him dead in his eyes and said, "I don't know what kind of women you are used to dating. But I will not regret this decision at all. As a matter of fact, I will be the one that you will never forget because I am the one who got away." I got in my car and drove away, not looking back, not even once ... And guess who called me the next day? I didn't bother to answer his call.

What do you think would have happened if I didn't know what I bring to the table; if I didn't know my value and my worth? I would have allowed someone into my life, someone into the most intimate part of me and he would not know how to treat me. How could he know how to treat me if he didn't take the time to know my value or my worth? I would have left feeling used and unhappy. The relationship could have possibly been all one-sided and definitely unfulfilling.

This is why it is so important that you know your worth. Knowing where you stand is empowering. You can begin to improve your own worth starting right now. Look in the mirror and take inventory of who you are; who God created you to be. Remind yourself of your worth and know that only those people who recognize your value and know how to handle and appreciate such a valuable asset such as yourself should be allowed into your life. You deserve nothing less.

"You can be the most beautiful person in the world and everybody sees light and rainbows when they look at you, but if you yourself don't know it, all of that doesn't even matter. Every second that you spend on doubting your worth, every moment that you use to criticize yourself; is a second of your life wasted, is a moment of your life thrown away. It's not like you have forever, so don't waste any of your seconds, don't throw even one of your moments away." ~ C. JoyBell C.

19 STOP MAKING EXCUSES FOR OTHERS' BAD BEHAVIOR

Stop making excuses for others' bad behavior. Stop settling and over compromising in your relationships just to feel accepted.

Stop making excuses for people! When people show you their true colors, don't try to paint a new picture.

Sometimes, we simply lie to ourselves. And that's just the truth. We lie to ourselves about the people we are around because we don't want to accept the fact that the people who we love, care for and spend so much time and energy trying to make happy ... well, they are really users, abusers and just all-around bad people. I've even seen some people hide behind the excuse that we must forgive each other. Yes, we must forgive each other, but we also must be accountable for our own individual actions. If someone is treating you poorly or not showing you the respect and care you know you deserve, don't just say:

> *Oh, it's okay. He was just having a bad day.*
> *She must be PMS-ing.*
> *He didn't really mean to say that.*
> *He just can't help himself.*

Each time you make up an excuse for a peoples' bad behavior, you are not holding them accountable for their actions. And consequently, you are teaching them that it is absolutely okay to treat you poorly or behave badly around you. When in reality, it is not. When you apply the lesson of setting boundaries from the previous section and start holding people accountable for the words that they say and their actions, you will begin to weed out the people who do not need to be in your life and begin surrounding yourself with higher quality people.

> *"If you want to surround yourself with quality people, stop making excuses for poor behavior and character flaws, especially when the acts are intentional and fully within their control." ~ Francisco Dao*

In almost all of my dating relationships, I sought acceptance and approval. I didn't know what I was doing then, but I can see clearly now. I approached every relationship as I do all things in life – anything worth having is worth working for. And I was taught that relationships take work. So I was ready and willing to roll up my sleeves and do the work – do all I could do – to make a relationship successful. I also walked into the relationship with the belief that if "I take care of you, you'll take care of me." So I did the work to make sure that my partner knew that I was there for him, that I had his back through thick and thin. I went out of my way to prove that I was supportive. That I was a team player: loving, kind, honest and faithful. I always made myself available to him. This usually did not work out in my favor. Why? Because I didn't receive the same treatment in return. While I was busy trying to prove my worth to a man, I never required him to do the same in return. I never required him to show me that he had my back, that he supported me, that he was a team player, that he was honest and kind. If he mistreated me, I made excuses for him such as, "He didn't mean to say that," or "He was really stressed today," or "Maybe I could have done something different/better."

I took his mistreatment of me to mean that I wasn't doing my part or working hard enough. Every single time, in every single relationship that I had this attitude, the relationship ended in heartbreak for me.

It wasn't until my broken engagement that I really did some soul searching and realized that I didn't know my worth. That I settled for less than what I know I deserved. Coming to this realization left me feeling somewhat embarrassed. Here I am a young, attractive woman with so much to offer and I never noticed it, nor did I surround myself with people who appreciated me. In that moment, I made a decision to change.

I made a decision to make sure that my words match my actions and my beliefs. Starting with my beliefs, I began to re-learn who I was and appreciate all my gifts and attributes. Having a good sense of who I was required that I only speak good things about myself. No more self-doubt. No more putting myself down. Knowing who I was and only speaking positivity about myself now required that I treat myself like I deserved. I no longer allowed people to talk to me in just any kind of way. I no longer surrounded myself with people who did not appreciate me. And I began to treat me the way I wanted to be treated. I began to take care of my mind, body and spirit the way that I would want someone else to take care of me.

At the end of the day, the only person you are responsible for is yourself. When you start demanding more of others, requiring others to treat you the way you want to be treated, there will be resistance. That's okay. It's not easy but you will be much better off to address these important issues rather than make excuses for them. It may be that they weren't meant to be in your life anyway. Only those who can like you, love you and accept you the way you are and treat you with love and respect deserve to be in your life. Nothing less.

REFLECTION

Use the lines below to express your thoughts and insights gained in this section. Describe how you can apply what you've learned in your everyday life.

_____

_____

_____

_____

_____

_____

_____

_____

_____

_____

_____

_____

_____

_____

_____

SECTION IV

THE MISFIT / NONCONFORMIST

20 LOVE AND ACCEPT YOURSELF JUST THE WAY YOU ARE

Don't deny or suppress anything. Accept yourself and others will do the same.

The misfit and outcast are very close cousins. They both struggle with their identity and are trying to fit in or be accepted. The key to finding your place in life is simply to love yourself just the way you are. When you don't love yourself or you don't accept the way you are, it shows in how you treat yourself and others. For the misfit, because you don't fit in with the norm, you tend to isolate yourself and shun everyone else. You may struggle between two thoughts: either you are not good enough for this world or the world is not good enough for you. When you focus on loving yourself, you understand that when you extend love and compassion to others, it is an extension of loving yourself. Instead of isolating yourself and going into hiding, come out in the open. Flaunt your beauty and the gifts you have that are uniquely yours. God did not create you to spend your life in hiding. God created you to be seen. So come out of hiding. Let others see you for who you are. Let others see you loving yourself just the way you are. When you let your light shine in the world, no matter if your light is blue, green or yellow, not only are you letting the world see your beauty, you are encouraging others to do the same. You never know who is watching you and whom you can positively influence.

How can you ask other people to love you and accept you for who you are when you can't even accept yourself? Be yourself, and don't mask who you are just because it's different. Remember there is only one like you. You are unique, beautiful, extraordinary. Don't change that.
~ Unknown

Most of my life, I've never felt as if I fit in with others my own age – no matter how much I wanted to. I didn't seem to fit into the different religious organizations I've explored. I didn't fit into the corporate world that I've been grooming myself for most of my adult life. I just didn't fit in. I think differently. I enjoy activities and hobbies that most 20-somethings don't engage in: the arts, ballroom dancing, theater, plays, and reading books on money, business and self-development. I don't look like everyone else: I dress conservatively (although with my own style ☺), I don't feel comfortable wearing tight clothes or showing a whole lot of skin (I can't remember when I wore shorts last – even with the heat of Houston). Not to mention that I look much younger than my age and I rarely wear makeup. I don't talk like everyone else (I enjoy talking about religion and politics, I enjoy healthy debates and exploring non-traditional topics such as metaphysics. I've even been made fun of for enunciating my words correctly and talking "country-proper"). Worst of all, I value relationships above all else. I enjoy developing close relationships with people. I enjoy being around those who I care about most and having a deep, meaningful relationship. All of these differences have really left me standing out from the crowd and seeking acceptance. But it wasn't until I hit my 30s that I really learned to love myself and like myself just the way I am. I stopped feeling sorry for myself and trying to fit in where I clearly didn't belong. There wasn't a "magical" moment when this happened: I just got tired. I got tired of trying to fit into an ideal of what people thought I should look like, act like or be like. When I was my true authentic self, I felt my best. So I decided to love me just the way I am.

I have learned to love every part of me – my personalities, my likes, my dislikes, my curves, my hair, my beauty marks, everything. God is perfect and I am wonderfully and beautifully made. Why should I wish I was different? Just so I could fit in? No, not anymore. I love me. I like me. And I'm not changing. Looking back, I really wished that I had as much self-love and confidence in my 20s as I do now – that's the only thing I would change. But once I started loving me from the inside out, I began to attract people who were similar to me, and form friendships and associations with people who think like me, who have similar hobbies and who talk like me. I am uniquely me, but there are others in the world who are close enough to being like me that I no longer feel lonely or out of place. I fit in just where I belong.

When you know yourself, you are empowered. When you accept yourself, you are invincible.

Celebrating what makes you special and letting your unique light shine isn't something that happens overnight. See it as a process, a series of baby steps rather than a big change that happens quickly. Be gentle with yourself – in this age of technology, we are inundated with social media updates. So often we get caught up in comparing our worst with someone else's best. Remind yourself that their gift is not yours to own and your gifts belong solely to you. You are you! Step up and shine knowing that it isn't about perfection, it's about being yourself and doing the best you can do.

21 KNOW YOUR WORTH

Don't shrink or belittle yourself for fear of intimidating others. You were created to be unique. You were created to shine.

> *You cannot blend in when you were meant to shine. Be a light.*

During the time when I was defining for myself who God was to me and what my religious beliefs were, I struggled a lot. I used to sit and wonder, *Why did I choose to be so different? Why does my brain function differently and just can't accept what it's been told without proof?* I felt like the black sheep of the family. Very few family members had encouraging words for me. I hadn't yet learned how to separate myself from the negativity, and instead, let it affect my self-esteem and my self-worth. There were times when I would lie to my family when asked, "Did you go to church this morning?" or "What church did you go to this morning?" I convinced myself that it was okay to lie for the sake of peace. But I did not have any peace. I had inner turmoil each time I decided to shrink back and not be the person God created me to be.

I realize now that I have done this all of my life. When I was a kid in school, people would say, "Oh, you're so smart." I would respond and say, "No, I just work hard." It was my way of downplaying my intelligence. Even as I grew into adulthood and started to date, I would downplay my career choice. When asked what I did for a living, I would say, "Oh, I work in the oil and gas industry." And quickly change the subject. I convinced myself that this was okay as a way to protect myself and to be more accepted by men (I believed that most men did not want a girl who was an engineer). But in reality, I did not show them who I really was. I did not show them I knew who I was and that I knew my worth. If I knew my worth, I wouldn't hide behind white lies and half-truths. If I knew my worth, I would say what I think and be proud of it. Dr. Seuss said it best ...

> *"Be who you are and say what you feel because those who mind don't matter and those who matter don't mind."* ~ **Dr. Seuss**

You are just the way God created you to be. God created you to be independent. God created you to think differently. God created you to stand out from the crowd. God created you to be unique. God created you to be an independent thinker. God makes no mistakes and He created you just the way you were meant to be. Yes, the pain of rejection that you are feeling is real. The pain and confusion of being different is real. This doesn't mean that there is something wrong with you. This is intentional, too. God created you to be a high quality diamond. Like most diamonds, everyone admires them and wants them. There are even some who may reject diamonds because they consider diamonds to be "out of their league." Diamonds are special and unique. If someone rejects a diamond, for whatever reason – it doesn't take away from the inherent value of the gem. You are not a cubic zirconia! You are a diamond. Tried by fire. Refined by the Master. Your sparkle and your shine are unique and brilliant. You can shine in any capacity

– all you have to do is stand tall, hold your head up high and take that first step toward being authentically you. The world doesn't need more of the same; the world needs more of you. As Oscar Wilde said, "Too many people die with their music still inside them." Never forget it.

"As we let our own light shine, we unconsciously give other people permission to do the same. As we are liberated from our fear, our presence automatically liberates others." ~ **Marianne Williamson**

22 BE PROUD OF YOURSELF

The reward for conformity is that everyone likes you but you.

It takes a tremendous amount of courage to be a nonconformist, to go against the status quo. At times, it can be absolutely scary to step out of the crowd and onto your own platform. But it is worth it. God will never give you more than what you can bear. So when He created you to be a nonconformist, He had already equipped you with the power, strength and courage to stand out on your own. When you harness your inner strength and embrace the person you were created to be, you begin to forge the path that you were designed to travel. You honor yourself and God when you embrace who you are and begin traveling the path that was meant only for you. Be proud of that. Be proud that God chose you. Be proud that God loves you so much that He gave you everything you need in order to walk the path less traveled. God chose you to be the pioneer. God chose you to be the leader. To be proud of yourself means to feel pleasure or satisfaction over something highly honorable about you. Embrace your journey. Embrace your path. Be proud of you. Be proud of the example and the leadership you are providing for others. The world needs you!

It's easy to stand with the crowd. It takes courage to stand alone.

Being proud of who you are doesn't always come easily. As a child, I was different than others. I grew up in a poor neighborhood in Memphis. My dad was a business owner, so that immediately made me "different." My parents were uber-religious and raised me as such, so that also made me stand out from the crowd. I was good with math and computers, so I was always the teacher's pet and the principal's favorite student. As a kid growing up, I didn't want this kind of recognition. I wanted to fit in. I wanted to be like everyone else. But as I grew older, I realized that being a misfit and a nonconformist was simply in my DNA. Being raised by really religious parents also meant being raised to fit into gender roles. That didn't quite work out for me. Not only did I excel in math and science (if you believed everything you read, girls, especially minority girls, shouldn't do well in these areas), I chose a nontraditional career. Not only did I choose a career in engineering, I chose a career in electrical engineering. According to the National Society of Professional Engineers, women are less likely to be employed in the fields of mechanical engineering and electrical engineering. And did I mention that my mom is a homemaker and my sisters are employed in traditional, female-dominated fields? My dad jokingly asked me once, "Are you sure you're my daughter?" I am proud of the choices that I have made because it has led me to a life that I could never have dreamed of. But I would not be here if I didn't have the courage to be a nonconformist. Because everything in life is a choice, I could have chosen a different road. I could have chosen to just be okay in math and science as a child. I could have chosen a traditional female career as a teacher or nurse or administrative assistant. I could have never left Memphis and stayed close to home until I married and had children. There is nothing wrong with women who choose this life, if this is their passion. But it wasn't my passion. My passion is math. My passion is science. My passion is helping people. My passion is traveling the world. My passion is so much bigger and grander than the traditional gender roles that I was raised with.

> *"People may hate you for being different and not living by society's standards, but deep down, they wish they had the courage to do the same."* ~ *Unknown*

You will feel pride in yourself when you find your purpose in life and pursue the goals you are passionate about. If you find yourself stuck, focus on finding a way out – refuse to give up on your dreams. Stand your ground when everyone else runs away and refuse to settle for less than what you deserve. Because I was courageous and stood up for who I am and what I want, because I was courageous enough to intentionally stand out from the crowd, I am now able to live a life that is better than what I dreamed of as a child. I love who I am and I love my life. And that makes it all worth it.

23 TREAT EVERYONE WITH RESPECT

"People take different roads seeking fulfillment and happiness. Just because they're not on your road doesn't mean they've gotten lost." ~ **H. Jackson Brown, Jr.**

Treat everyone with respect. As a misfit, you stand out from the crowd. But just because you don't fit in with the crowd doesn't give you the right to look down on the crowd or be disrespectful toward them or their beliefs. God has a purpose for all of us, whether we go with the grain or against the grain. We all have a purpose. We all have a journey to take. We all have a final destination. We may have similar goals and similar destinations. However, how we travel and what road we choose to take is an individual decision.

In today's society, we are so focused on who's right and who's wrong that we end up sacrificing relationships in the name of ego. This is especially true in religion. I can only speak for Christianity, but I believe that this is one of the reasons why many people have pulled away from traditional church and Christian practices. The Christian religion has been divided into several denominations. I grew up in one denomination that believed that if you were not a member of this one denomination, you were not a true Christian and, therefore, you were condemned to hell. And all throughout my childhood experience, I was inundated with a continuous list of everything that every other church and denomination was doing wrong – which is why they couldn't be true Christians. But what my church failed to realize is that while they were so focused on proving everyone else wrong, they forgot about the true message of Christ, and that was to spread the love of God. I have been witness to so-called preachers and elders having Bible study with people who were not members of this denomination and hearing these people referred to as "stupid" or "ignorant" or some other demeaning and demoralizing word. Behavior like this does not serve Christ or Christianity. And this behavior does not show love. I have seen relationships destroyed because of destructive words and behaviors. In the end, none of the people who were verbally attacked, ridiculed or disrespected ever became members of this denomination. If these people ever came around, it was always under the agreement that religion would not be discussed. And that was for the few who did not run out the door, never to return.

"It is not our differences that divide us. It is our inability to recognize, accept, and celebrate those differences."
~ Audre Lorde

We cannot accomplish anything in this world without relationships. Destroying relationships to prove you're right and the other person is wrong does not accomplish anything. The golden rule of life states "Do unto others as you would have them do unto you." This means to treat everyone the way you want to be treated. Your goal on earth is not to convince others that your ideals, goals and vision are better than everyone else. Your goal on earth is to live your life to the fullest by using your gifts to add value to the world around you. So be kind. Treat everyone with the same respect you want to be given. Don't ridicule others for being a conformist or a "sheep." Treat everyone with gentleness, love and mercy. Treating people with respect makes this world a nicer place. God created this earth with people made up of a wide variety of cultures, backgrounds and lifestyles. If you treat others with respect, your journey through life will be easier, it will be more interesting and you will also gain the respect of those around you.

> *"What we have to do ... is to find a way to celebrate our diversity and debate our differences without fracturing our communities."* ~ **Hillary Clinton**

24 Continue to Learn and Grow

Keep exploring. Connect with others. Share your discoveries. Deepen your understanding.

If you are like me, you may have become a misfit because you love to learn and explore new things. In that case, learning has always been a part of your life. But as you start to develop your belief system and choose which path to follow, you may begin to think that you know all there is to know because you have a chosen path. On the contrary. Your learning is just beginning. Learning is a lifelong process – no matter what path you have chosen. Your path may contain mountains, valleys, twists and turns. Your path will lead you to meet a great number of people from different cultures and socio-economic backgrounds.

As you travel, you will discover new and exciting things: your understanding of the world around you will grow deeper and more complex. You must be open to learning. If you close your mind off to learning new things or seeing things from a different perspective, you risk losing growth, understanding, appreciation and beauty. When you close your mind off to learning new things, your path can become quite boring because you already know everything your path was designed to teach you. Where's the fun in that? Where's the excitement in that? Your life was not designed to be boring, all one level, with no room for growth. Every living thing on this planet experiences growth either physically or intellectually (adaptation/mutation) or both. If it is alive, it will grow – from the smallest microorganism to the tallest tree. You can do the same.

When I decided to no longer follow the religious beliefs that I was taught growing up, I had to decide what I wanted to believe. In order to decide, I had to learn new things. So I read my Bible. I read books. I visited different churches. I talked to different people. I learned about other religions. Some people assumed that just because I was stretching my horizons and learning so much about different churches and religions that I was lost and I was just accepting everything that people told me or what I read. I often heard the phrase, "Don't be so open-minded that your brain falls out." The truth is that I am open-minded. Another truth is that in all of my learning, I have gained an understanding and appreciation for everyone else. Just because you know something doesn't mean that you have to believe it and apply it to your life. There are people in the world who believe that they can walk on fire and can drink poison without dying. They believe this. I know this. But it doesn't mean that I will choose to believe it as well. However, I can respect them without agreeing with them. And this is what allows us to live in harmony with one another. So when I finally defined my religious beliefs, I was confident and sure in my beliefs, while at the same time respectful of the other religions of the world.

Never stop learning, because life never stops teaching.

So keep on learning. Keep on exploring. Follow your spirit when choosing which path to follow and store all the other knowledge you've gained as reference material for awesome coffee conversations.

"Anyone who stops learning is old, whether at twenty or eighty. Anyone who keeps learning stays young. The greatest thing in life is to keep your mind young." ~ **Henry Ford**

It was Gandhi who said, "Learn as if you were to live forever." Our time here on earth is very limited, in the grand scheme of things. God knows this and that is why He planted in each of us the seed of curiosity. We are not meant to stop growing and learning. Part of walking your path is allowing yourself to experience new things. As we get older, it can be more difficult to do this. However, there are a few ways you can jump-start your own intellectual growth:

- Surround yourself with achievers. Seek out those individuals who are growing and learning; you'll find inspiration in sharing your life with them and experiencing their accomplishments, even if it is just vicariously.

- Turn off the technology and relax your mind. Even just turning off the TV and using that time to read or learn a new skill will expand your horizons.

- Become a mentor to someone else. One of the best ways to learn is to teach someone else.

- Be interested in meeting new people. The next time you go to the post office or stand in line at the grocery store, talk to those people around you. Maintaining this habit of curiosity about others will keep your mind open and receptive to new things.

- Create something; it's a great way to express what you've learned.

Once you've put some of these ideas into practice, you'll soon find that your brain, heart and soul will be begging to learn something new and you'll be learning and growing every day.

25 FOLLOW THE ROAD LESS TRAVELED

The Road Not Taken

TWO roads diverged in a yellow wood,
And sorry I could not travel both
And be one traveler, long I stood
And looked down one as far as I could
To where it bent in the undergrowth;

Then took the other, as just as fair,
And having perhaps the better claim,
Because it was grassy and wanted wear;
Though as for that the passing there
Had worn them really about the same,

And both that morning equally lay
In leaves no step had trodden black.
Oh, I kept the first for another day!
Yet knowing how way leads on to way,
I doubted if I should ever come back.

I shall be telling this with a sigh
Somewhere ages and ages hence:
Two roads diverged in a wood, and I –
I took the one less traveled by,
And that has made all the difference.

~ Robert Frost(1874–1963)

Each day that you and I wake up, we have a decision to make: Will I follow the crowd and do what everyone else is doing? Or will I be true to myself, follow my spirit and possibly choose a different path? This is the question that I asked myself when I decided to go into business for myself. As often as you hear about people becoming entrepreneurs, actually becoming an entrepreneur is not a popular choice for many. Many prefer the sense of comfort and stability offered by companies in corporate America. Many people prefer having set hours to start work and end work, and a job that is the same Monday through Friday. And very few people get excited about the level of responsibility and accountability required of an entrepreneur. Although my parents owned their own business (albeit a struggling business), deciding to start my own company wasn't an easy choice. Very few of my friends and family members had aspirations of starting their own businesses. And those who did start a business did so for the tax write-off. But I wanted to start a business to change the world. However, such a large vision would require of me an equally large sacrifice (in time, money and effort). And I wasn't ready for that. Instead, I chose to do what everyone else was doing and start MLM businesses (multi-level marketing). The experience in MLM was great, but it did not lead me down the path that my heart desired. It wasn't until I decided to start my company from the ground up, creating the vision, creating the products, marketing my products and services ... it wasn't until I followed my heart and followed my vision that I became fulfilled. Very few people are willing to step out on the edge and start a company from the ground up to support their mission and their business. That's the allure of MLMs. MLMs have done all the groundwork for you. But I wanted something different. So I did something different.

I encourage you to choose the road less traveled. Choose something different for yourself if that is where your heart is leading you. You only have one life to live. Why spend your time doing what everyone else does only to end up unfulfilled? If you find that the majority is headed in one direction, consider what would happen if you went the other way. Have the self-confidence in yourself and faith in God to step out and follow your vision. Don't be afraid to bet on yourself – go all in – even if the path you've chosen is less obvious to most. When you choose to follow your own path, more often than not, you will find it makes all the difference in the world.

26 Be Peaceful

*Seek peace and pursue it. ~ **Psalm 34:14***

Too many people misinterpret the misfit for being a trouble-maker. This isn't always the case. Although you may ask questions and disagree with the status quo, never let your words or actions be the cause of a chaotic situation. "Let your conversation be always full of grace, seasoned with salt ..."

You do not have to go around convincing others that your chosen path is THE path. Choose to let your conversation be filled with love and grace. When someone wants to engage you in conversation, simply engage them. Share with them your story and your decision-making process. Your goal is simply to share, not to convince.

I enjoy a good debate as much as the next person. But I have learned that conversations can quickly go from a friendly and fun debate to a hot and intense argument, especially on topics such as race, politics and religion. During my last semester in college, one of my classmates decided to have a pool party for our class. This particular class only had around 10 students (this was a graduate course). I noticed that everyone received an invitation except for me. I didn't ask about it. But the student decided to approach me and explain to me why I didn't get an invitation. He said that he was having the party at a friend's house and his friend did not like for black people to be in his pool because we make the pool dirtier. ... (crickets) ... (blank stare) ...

At this point, I had a choice to make about how I was going to respond. It is a fact that I am black. And it is a fact that I was the only black student in class. So I was a misfit by pure design, not by choice. I could have gotten into a really heated argument with this student and explained to him how wrong he and his friend were on so many levels. Or I could choose to keep the peace. I chose to keep the peace. In a very calm, but authoritative voice, I informed this student that his friend was simply wrong about black people. Black people are naturally dry, which is why we always have to use lotion and Vaseline to keep our skin hydrated. It is also why we cannot wash our hair every day. Our bodies simply do not produce the oil that our Caucasian counterparts do. So in actuality, a Caucasian brings more dirt and oil into his friends' pool than I ever could. And I just simply walked away. At the end of the day, I still had his respect (to a certain extent) and he had no cause to drag my name through the mud or ruin my reputation. Had I decided to respond in a less-than-peaceful manner, I would have done more damage to myself than I would have done to him.

Becoming peaceful is a choice and it will take an effort to choose peace in your everyday life. The next time you are confronted for being different physically or intellectually, think about your response. Respond with intellect instead of emotion. When you respond with intellect, you will not only preserve your image and your reputation, but you will plant a seed of growth in the other person's mind. Once you begin to experience the benefits in your life and in the lives of those around you, you'll want to keep on making peace.

> *"Peace is not absence of conflict, it is the ability to handle conflict by peaceful means."* ~ ***Ronald Reagan***

27 Seek Spiritual Alignment and Acceptance

*Seek God's will in all that you do and He will direct your paths. ~ **Proverbs 3:6***

God will not put more on you than what you can bear. Whatever you are going through, God has already equipped you with the strength you need to make it through.

*"Silence can bring us into alignment with our thoughts and feelings and help us to hear the quiet spiritual voice of our intuition." ~ **Michael Thomas Sunnarborg***

This is what really makes you a misfit. God has given you specific gifts, talents, ways of thinking and a path to travel that set you apart from everyone else. God has given you a special kind of strength, a special kind of tenacity that others do not have. But in order to fully grasp this, you have to be intentional about your spiritual alignment with God. Being a misfit isn't just about being different for the heck of it. You have a purpose. God has a specific plan for your life and your gifts. But you have to find out what it is. Relying on yourself to figure it out will only lead you around in circles and get you nowhere at all. When you are a misfit, conventional ways of doing things (the status quo) will not work for you.

We may seek God by our intellect, but we only can find Him with our heart.

There were so many nights when I cried myself to sleep, wondering why God made me so different. I used to think that I was too sensitive and my heart was weak. I thought that I loved too hard, I was too compassionate and I loved too easily. It seemed each time I followed my heart, I ended up getting hurt. I seriously questioned God about why He made me this way. Why was I so sensitive? Why did I make decisions from the heart? Why was I the one always getting hurt? Why couldn't I be like everyone else and make decisions like everyone else (from the head, not the heart)? Why? Why? Why? It wasn't until I actually stopped asking 'why' long enough to hear from God that I began to understand why I was made to go against the grain. God knew that I had to have a combination of sensitivity and logic in order to travel down the path I was meant to travel. God knew that I needed to experience the hurt and disappointment in order to learn the lessons I needed. Now, even after that revelation, I still ask God, "Um, couldn't I have just read that in a book instead of having to actually experience all of this?" I think God just laughed at me and shook His head. He does have a great sense of humor – I am living proof!

Sometimes, we have to go through growing pains of understanding who we are and WHY we are. It is a process. But you have to allow God into the process. God is able to show you the answers to your questions through prayer and meditation. Don't go through life trying to figure it all out on your own. Ask God questions and wait for His answers. He will reveal them to you if you earnestly seek Him.

"You seek the heights of manhood when you seek the depths of God." ~ **Edwin Louis Cole**

I have found that there are a few ways I can check in to ensure that I am seeking God's will for my life:

1. Ask yourself: What do I really want? Listen for the answer and write it down. You'll be amazed at how often we plow through life thinking we know the answer to that question, but never really find the answer. Take the time to listen for God's response.

2. Are you truly seeking God's kingdom first? Only you can know your true motives. Are your desires living up to God's priorities or to your own?

3. Are you pursuing wisdom? Have you sought wise counsel? Seek a variety of opinions from those who have been there, done that. This will give you some clarity. Also, spend time reading His Word and gaining knowledge from scripture. After all, God promises to be a lamp to your feet and a light to your path!

Once you've asked yourself these questions and taken time to listen to the answers, you should have all you need to know about God's will for your life.

REFLECTION

Use the lines below to express your thoughts and insights gained in this section. Describe how you can apply what you've learned in your everyday life.

_____

_____

_____

_____

_____

_____

_____

_____

_____

_____

_____

_____

_____

_____

_____

SECTION V

THE LOGICAL THINKER

28 Allow Your Heart and Your Head to Work Together

Follow your heart because if you always trust your mind, you'll always act on logic, and logic doesn't always lead to happiness...

Invite your heart into the decision-making process. I know, I know. You're looking at me right now asking, "Why in the world would I want to invite my heart into this process?" Well, let me ask you a question. In your car, do you have different tools to help you drive and navigate so that you can reach your destination safely? What would happen if I took away your rearview and sideview mirrors? You would have a difficult time backing up and changing lanes, wouldn't you? You could accidentally run into someone because you didn't have your mirrors there to support you. Taking your heart out of the process works the same way. You were equipped with a mind and a heart to help you navigate this thing called life. When you only use part of the tools you were given, your journey becomes more difficult and "accident prone." But if you use all of the tools you were given in the way that they were meant to be used, your journey through life will be much more efficient, enjoyable and have fewer accidents (or mistakes).

Your heart is like any other muscle or tool. You must use it. The more you use it, the stronger and more reliable it will become. Trust your heart. If you leave your heart up on the shelf unused, it will begin to atrophy. If you don't use your heart much in your decision-making, that may be why it feels so foreign to you. It's been on the shelf for too long and it's barely recognizable to the eyes or to the touch. You have got to use your heart. Your heart is smarter and stronger than what you give it credit for.

Be sure to take your heart off of the shelf. Examine it. Listen to it. Learn all of the functions of your heart. Learn all of its quirks. There are cracks in your heart. Understand the source of those cracks. And if necessary, super glue the parts back together. Those cracks have just added character and wisdom to your heart. So you definitely want to know them and keep them.

Once you've gotten to know your heart, allow your heart and your head to work together. You can be both logical and heart-conscious at the same time. Your heart and your head work together to bring balance to you and to your life. Continuing to operate on one without the other will not bring you peace and happiness.

> *The human heart feels things the eyes cannot see and knows what the mind cannot understand.*

For so many years, I tried to silence my heart. I just didn't trust it. My heart was too abstract, too soft for my taste. I like things to be solid and concrete. So I tried to be logical and mental about everything. But in doing so, I ignored sound advice and warnings that my inner spirit wanted to tell me.

When I got married, I did not listen to my heart. I chose to be logical – thinking that if I were logical, he would be logical too and abide by the rules of logic. Logic, to me, meant happiness. I believed that if a person said that he loves you, he wouldn't lie to you. I believed that if I invested my time and energy into someone when he was down, he would return the favor and invest his time and energy into me. I believed that if I loved someone with all of my heart, he would love me with all of his heart. After all, that makes sense, right? You get in what you put out, right? A + B = C, right?

Wrong. I chose not to listen to my heart and that decision came with a cost.

When my heart spoke to me and told me something wasn't right, I ignored it, mistaking my intuition for fear. My heart nudged me when my ex told me lies. But I ignored it because a person who loves you wouldn't lie to you, right? My heart became extremely uncomfortable when I began investing more into the relationship than what I was receiving, reasoning within myself that there were times in every relationship when one person gives more than the other, and this was just my turn to give. My heart cried tears of pain and disappointment when his words didn't match his actions while my brain rationalized that men are just sometimes like that. They are rough around the edges and need to be taught how to treat a woman ... I was determined not to let what I called "fear" (which was really my heart speaking) keep me from having a loving relationship ...

In reality, my heart was screaming that I wasn't in a loving relationship. If I had only invited my heart and my head to be in the equation together, I could have saved myself time, energy, money and heartbreak.

> *"By all means, follow your heart. Just be sure to take your brains with you."* ~ **Unknown**

The next time you want to be able to make the most balanced decision, invite your heart in to collaborate with your logical brain. First, take a deep breath and connect with your body. As you exhale, ask yourself what you are feeling. Go deeper with each breath and you may feel a gentle tug toward the best direction. Next, trust yourself. Only you know what's best for you, so put all of your resources to work together to help you make the choices you need to make on your journey through life. Sometimes you have to let go and experience life. The choices you make are never wrong – there is always something to learn or new ways to grow. Know that God only wants the best for you.

29 ALIGN YOUR HEART, MIND AND SPIRIT

"Quiet the mind, and the soul will speak." ~ Ma Jaya Sati Bhagavati

Now that you have learned to include your heart, you must now bring all parts of yourself into play. You already trust your mind and your own logic. You have learned how to trust your heart. Now, you must learn to trust your intuition. It will never fail you. Your intuition is your heart and your spirit working together. But you must learn to be still, be quiet and live in the present to fully align your heart and your spirit. Those of us who are engineer-type people have a hard time sitting still and quieting our minds because we are always thinking and planning. But trust me, with a lot of discipline and hard work (which, I'm sure you are familiar with) it can be done. The good news is that sometimes your intuition will be logical. Sometimes it won't. Just because it is not logical doesn't mean that it is wrong. When your heart and your spirit are in **alignment**, it can never steer you wrong.

You have to be intentional about aligning your heart, mind and spirit. Alignment doesn't come easily or naturally in a world filled with distractions. And it certainly doesn't come easily to the person whose mind is always moving, thinking and planning. So be intentional. First, decide that it can be done. Then, believe that you have the spirit of God within you. And because you have the spirit of God within you, you can trust your spirit and choose to trust your spirit (you have the power of choice). Finally, meditate. Listen to the reasoning of your mind. Feel the expressions of your heart. And follow the guidance of your spirit.

The quieter you become, the more you can hear.

Finding time to be still and quiet was always a challenge for me. I liked being busy and I liked being productive. So the only time I was still and quiet was when I was asleep. When I chose to marry my ex-husband, I ignored my heart and my spirit. At the time, I prayed and asked God if this is who I should marry. But I never sat still long enough to listen for his response. It wasn't until after I was married and became absolutely miserable that I learned the importance of being still. Because we have the spirit of God within us – when there are really important messages that we need to hear, our spirit will find a way to deliver it to us. My spirit spoke to me through my dreams. I was in a state of desperation before I was open enough to allow my spirit to speak to me through my dreams. I received many of the answers that I sought while I slept. Once it dawned on me that I needed to be in a state of stillness and quietness, I began to be intentional about listening for the voice of God. I had to learn that I could not engineer every single aspect of my life alone. I needed the input and advice of my spirit in order to design the life that I knew I deserved. Once I began to not only pray to God, but to listen to my spirit, I became more effective in applying my logic and my heart to every situation.

"Prayer is your speaking to God. Meditation is allowing the spirit to speak to you." ~ Deepak Chopra

Aligning your heart, mind and spirit takes practice and consistent effort. When you find yourself getting ahead of God's plans for you, take a moment to slow down and allow your sprit to show you the guidance you seek. If you need inspiration, take a walk and soak in the beauty of the season. While you walk, appreciate the spirit of nature and notice its perfect order. Nature is an excellent example of alignment!

30 You Must Let Go in Order to Fall Into Place

I know what I'm doing. I have it all planned out – plans to take care of you, not abandon you, plans to give you the future you hope for. ~ *Jeremiah* **29:11** *(MSG)*

Letting go was by far the hardest lesson I've ever had to learn. But it was a necessary lesson. I learned that letting go is not a free fall. What does it mean to let go? To let go means releasing the pressure from yourself to have every single detail of your life planned and mapped out. I was bad about this.

I am the master planner. I can plan anything and everything. I've had plans for my life since I was a little girl. Even through adulthood, I've always had a plan. If I didn't have a plan, I felt completely lost. Don't get me wrong, some plans are good. I still use my calendar religiously. And when my life gets really hectic, I have to plan and schedule time for everything from meditation to grocery shopping. But for the bigger plans of my life, I use pencil instead of a pen to mark my calendar. Letting go of the responsibility to not only have a plan but to have the RIGHT or PERFECT plan has released so much pressure.

When you are not stressed, you become free to think clearly and operate more effectively in the present. You become free to follow your inner spirit as you encounter unforeseen circumstances. In the past, when something unforeseen would happen, I would stop everything, literally, and go back to the drawing board to re-work the plan or create a new plan to handle the new situation. Now, when something unforeseen happens, I pause instead of stopping. I take time to recognize what is happening, and then follow my inner spirit on what to do next, even if the next step isn't necessarily in line with my original plans. When I follow my inner spirit, the results are either:

- a bigger lesson learned
- a presentation of a new/better opportunity that I did not see before, or
- a bigger impact than I thought I could have had

The more I practice letting go and letting God, the easier it gets. I still have my plans, but I am not as attached to my plans as I used to be. I surrender my plans over to God and let God steer me. When a change in direction comes, all I do is take out my eraser, erase what I had planned, and replace it with the new God-given plan. You have the spirit of God within you (your inner spirit). When you listen to your spirit and your heart, you will never be led wrong.

God has a bigger plan for me than I have for myself.

A few short years after my marriage ended, I found myself in love again and ready to give marriage another try. The man that I had been dating proposed to me and I said, "Yes." We went through the normal steps of seeking premarital counseling and "doing the work" before we said, "I do." In my opinion, things were going well. Yes, we had our ups and downs, but nothing that I consid-ered a dealbreaker. And this relationship was 10 times better than my previous relationship. But, unbeknownst to me, things weren't going as well as they seemed. After an argument, I received an email from him saying that he didn't think we should be married and that he would have his things moved out by the weekend. I was all kinds of hurt and upset. For one thing, I didn't think the argument we just had was worth breaking up over. Two, who breaks up over email? Three, one day you're ready to marry me, and the next day you're not? So after a heart-wrenching talk, we decided that we would call off the engagement, and work on the relationship. Sounds like a good solution, right? He made requests of me and I made requests of him. And for a few weeks, things were going good again. We were laughing again. And suddenly, out of the blue, he told me, "It's not you, it's me." He walked out and I haven't seen him since. He completely broke my heart – AGAIN.

And if you recall the story from Chapter 17, I lost a close girlfriend around the same time as my relationship with my then boyfriend/fiancé ended.

I couldn't understand why this was happening to me. The man whom I loved and cared for deeply decided that he didn't want to marry me. The woman that I considered as one of my closest friends was no longer treating me as a friend – but as her enemy. The thing that I value most – relationships – was being taken away from me

I was completely lost. I had no idea what to do, how to do it or when to do it. I usually have a plan. I usually have a backup plan to the main plan – and a backup plan to the backup plan. But this time I was empty. I had no ideas. I had nowhere to turn and no one to turn to. I was alone. But it was in this moment of broken-heartedness that I became completely vulnerable. Between the crying, the praying and the reading of my Bible, it dawned on me that I was still depending on myself. I hadn't completely surrendered to God and before this time, I hadn't diligently sought His will. In all of my plan-making, I did not align my spirit with the will of God. I made my plans, and then asked God to bless my plans. I did not involve God in the planning process or even ask Him, "What would you have me to do?" "Where would you have me to go?" It dawned on me that I was still relying on myself.

In that moment, I decided to let go. Faith knows that things are going to work out, even when I don't know HOW they are going to work out. In the quietness of that hotel room, my spirit reaffirmed to me that God created me. God knows how much of a thinker and a planner I am. God is not going to leave me hanging without any signs or direction. God wouldn't do that because that is not how He created me. So through the tears and the loneliness, I made this declaration:

> *I declared that I trust God. I trust that God will lead me and guide me in all things. God will show me which direction to go. In the process, God will show me just enough of the next step or two, but in order to build my faith muscles, He will not show me everything until I learn to completely trust Him.*

God will always work things out in my favor just the way they need to be worked out. So, while I didn't know how I was going to heal, and I didn't know how I was going to move on, I only knew that I would. And true to God-like form, I began to heal. I began to move. And true to my declaration, God began to show me the next couple of steps that I needed to take.

Since that time, life has gotten better and better because I learned to let go and let God, knowing that God is a God of order, not confusion. God has a plan just like I do. I just needed to trust His plans as much as I trust my own.

Now that I know that God has a plan, and that God's plans are for good, not disaster, to give me a future and hope – and I see that life has proven these things to be so – it has become much easier for me to let God co-pilot life with me. Allowing God to lead me and guide me has led me to much better plans than anything I could have come up with myself.

It was only when I planned to let go that I actually gained more control and created a better life.

> *God has a perfect plan for us. He never does it all at once,*
> *just step by step because he wants to teach us to walk by*
> *faith not by sight.*

You don't know what you're going to face this week, but I can tell you that God knows. And He wants you to let go and let Him be in control. Consider that most of your stress comes when you are in conflict with God – when you are trying to take control of your life from Him. The more you do that, the more you are trying to play God, which puts you in opposition to God. This will only leave you frustrated and tired.

The last eight lines of the Serenity Prayer capture the importance of letting go: "Living one day at a time, enjoying one moment at a time, accepting hardship as a pathway to peace, taking as Jesus did this sinful world as it is, not as I would have it; trusting that You will make all things right if I surrender to Your will so that I may be reasonably happy in this life and supremely happy with You forever in the next. Amen."

31 CHOOSE LOVE OVER FEAR

There is no fear in love; but perfect love casts out fear, because fear involves torment. But he who fears has not been made perfect in love. ~ *1 John 4:18*

Knowing that you have the spirit of God within you, and that there is nothing impossible for God, you should rest assured that there is nothing to fear. Fear and love cannot coexist. God is love. Choose love (God) over fear every day.

Fear is a powerful thing. Some would even argue that fear is the most powerful emotion that humans ever experience. Fear causes us to become stagnate and stuck. Fear causes us to panic and act irrationally. Fear may even cause us to miss our blessing when it comes to us in unexpected ways.

The only thing more powerful than fear is love. But just like everything else in life, we must choose love over fear every day and in every situation. How do you choose love? You choose love by choosing God. You choose love by listening to the spirit of God within you. You choose love by believing that everything works together for your good. You choose love by believing that God only has plans to prosper you, not to harm you. You choose love by thinking about all the things that could go right, instead of all the things that could go wrong. You choose love by finding a quiet space, turning within yourself for prayer and meditation, and asking God to reveal to you what you should do. Because God is love, his answers and direction to you will guide you down the path of love.

> *"There are two basic motivating forces: fear and love. When we are afraid, we pull back from life. When we are in love, we open to all that life has to offer with passion, excitement, and acceptance. We need to learn to love ourselves first, in all our glory and our imperfections. If we cannot love ourselves, we cannot fully open to our ability to love others or our potential to create. Evolution and all hopes for a better world rest in the fearlessness and open-hearted vision of people who embrace life."* ~ **John Lennon**

Have you ever read "The Alchemist"? One of the running themes in this story is how the main character, Santiago, overcomes fear and how some of the other characters allow fear to take over and limit their lives.

The Danger of Fear

Fear persistently comes up throughout Santiago's journey as the primary obstacle to Santiago's successfully achieving his Personal Legend. Santiago experiences several forms of fear: a childhood fear of having the gypsy woman interpret his dream; a material fear of losing his wealth by departing to Tangier or by joining the desert caravan; the physical fear of dying in the battle at Al-Fayoum; and the spiritual fear that he will fail to turn himself into the wind when the alchemist forces him to try.

Santiago's mentors, from Melchizedek to the alchemist,

condemn fear by comparing it to materialism, and they describe it as a product of misunderstanding how the universe treats those pursuing their Personal Legends. Fear, they suggest, should become irrelevant, even in the face of death, if you faithfully pursue your dreams.

Source: SparkNotes 2014

Have you ever felt like Santiago: having fears of different people and situations from times past or from times yet to come? At some point, all of us have experienced fear. What you do with that fear is the key. There have been times in my life where I was afraid to ask for what I wanted in relationships, afraid to pursue unconventional paths in religion, or afraid of traveling alone. But when I was in the midst of these fears, the one thing that I forgot was the love of God. When you are mentally, spiritually and emotionally aligned, you are aligned with the love of God. The love of God gives you assurance that He will lead you and guide you down the right path. The love of God gives you assurance that He will protect you. The love of God assures you that everything is working together for your good. Fear wants you to forget this. Fear is not of God, so it opposes everything that God is – including love. But once I was reminded of the love of God, I was able to break away from the stronghold that fear had on me. I am no longer afraid to ask for what I want and need from my relationships. I am no longer afraid of rejection from peers by pursuing unconventional paths. I am no longer afraid of traveling alone to experience the magnificence of God's earth. Just like Santiago in "The Alchemist," I had to do the work of intentionally choosing the love of God over fear. In doing so, I learned that the things that I feared the most were least likely to happen. And of the worst things that could happen, I could always recover from them. So, what is there really to fear?

"Our deepest fear is not that we are inadequate. Our deepest fear is that we are powerful beyond measure. It is our light, not our darkness that most frightens us. We ask ourselves, 'Who am I to be brilliant, gorgeous, talented, fabulous?' Actually, who are you not to be? You are a child of God. Your playing small does not serve the world. There is nothing enlightened about shrinking so that other people won't feel insecure around you. We are all meant to shine, as children do. We were born to make manifest the glory of God that is within us. It's not just in some of us; it's in everyone. And as we let our own light shine, we unconsciously give other people permission to do the same. As we are liberated from our own fear, our presence automatically liberates others." ~ **Marianne Williamson**

The human brain is hard-wired for fear: we all have an amygdala, the brain mechanism that triggers a fight or flight response. In that way, fear will always be around; however, you can re-interpret how you respond to fear. Instead of allowing fear to trigger negative feelings, think of it as an ally. Those fear- filled moments can offer you clarity and light that give you a chance to choose love. Think of fear as a loving messenger – an opportunity to sit up and take notice rather than run or hide.

32 You Control Your Thoughts. Your Thoughts do not Control You

"He who controls his own thoughts, controls his own destiny." ~ Ross Arntson

As logical thinkers, we tend to be in our heads a lot. We like to think about all of the possibilities. But sometimes, when we are in our heads so much, we entertain nonproductive thoughts. We think about all of the things that could go wrong. We overthink a situation. Sometimes, we get so caught up in our thoughts that we never take action, or we make things worse than they really are.

You must be intentional with your thoughts. You must take control of what you think about on a regular basis. What you think about affects how you feel and what you do. If your mind is always focused on a meteorite falling from the sky and hitting your house, what will happen? Because you are so intent on thinking about this event, your heart will be filled with fear and your thoughts will focus on protecting yourself and your family. And because your thoughts are so intent on this meteorite, fear and protection, you will then begin to build or purchase something to protect yourself and your family.

Simply put – Thoughts become things. Thoughts become action.

If you are wondering why you can't seem to make progress in a certain area of your life, or why you feel unhappy, or why your relationships are suffering, take a look at your thoughts. What are you thinking about?

To be intentional about your thoughts means to only think about what you want to think about. If you want a different or better job, then the majority of your thoughts should be spent thinking about that new job. Not thinking about how much you hate your current job.

Whatever you water will grow.

If you are constantly thinking about that new job you want – you think about what the first day will be like, how you will feel, the salary you will earn, the responsibilities you will have – and constantly thinking about these things all day, every day, your mind will then begin to create plans to help you achieve your goal. When you think so intently on something so positive, you create a desire so strong that your daily actions and decisions will begin to reflect and move you toward your goals.

However, the opposite is also true. If you constantly think about how much you hate your job – you hate the drive to work, you hate your cubicle, you strongly dislike your boss and co-workers – constantly thinking about these things day in and day out will create such a negative impact on your mind that any action you take will also be negative and continue to keep your life in a negative state.

Be intentional.

Choose your thoughts.

Think about all the things you want in your life, how you will feel and how you will bless others with these things. Think about these things more than you think about anything else and you will be sure to create the best life for you.

> *"You are today where your thoughts have brought you; you will be tomorrow where your thoughts take you."* ~ *James Allen*

Personally, I have experienced the power of being intentional about my thoughts. When I first heard the notion that thoughts create things and can change your life, I was skeptical. So one day, I just decided to pay attention to the things that I was thinking. What I noticed about myself shocked me. I noticed that most of my thoughts were negative. I've always had a vivid imagination. So throughout any given day, I would allow my imagination to run wild with more negative thoughts than positive thoughts. Before I got out of bed to go to work, I would daydream about how terrible the day would be, what unreasonable request I would be asked to do and how satisfying it would feel to just go in and "bless" everyone out! The results? I had a miserable day. My day was just as I expected it to be. I went to work in a less-than-positive attitude. People made me angry or rubbed me the wrong way because I was already in a funky mood. And the day just continued to go downhill.

Then I tried an experiment. I decided that the next day, I would be intentional about thinking how I wanted my day to go. So when I woke up – old habits die hard – I started thinking about all the things that I hated about getting up at 4 a.m. to go to work. But then I caught myself. I changed my thoughts to think about the good that I wanted to happen. I began to think about how thankful I was to have a job that pays well and that I have reliable transportation to get me to and from work. I started thinking to myself about how productive my day was going to be. I thought about what work I wanted to get accomplished and how good it would feel to have these accomplishments. I started thinking about how certain co-workers got on my nerves – but I decided that this was just the way that they are. So if they approached me with nonsense, I'd find something to laugh about or crack a joke or talk about the weather ... I thought about exactly the way I wanted my day to go and how I wanted to react in a positive or productive way. And guess what happened? My day was so much better than the previous day. I didn't go to work with a funky attitude – so it wasn't so easy for people to get on my nerves or rub me the wrong way. And the people who normally got on my nerves didn't bother me as much – I held my peace, accepted them for who they are, and directed my energy into something that would make me laugh (sometimes I simply think – thank you God that I am not married to this person!).

The same is true for my business. When I first started my business, I was very intentional with my thoughts. I spent dedicated time (in the morning and in the evenings) to concentrate and think only thoughts of what I want my business to be like and how I wanted to run my company. I thought intently about the people I wanted to meet and collaborate with and the people who I wanted to help with my product and services. I spent hours each day thinking, imagining and feeling all of the positive possibilities that I wanted to happen in my life. Did everything work out exactly how I imagined it or when I wanted it to happen? No, it didn't. However, every day that I am intentional, I create a positive day with positive results that move me in the direction of the very thing that I am thinking about and praying about.

> *"Self-discipline begins with the mastery of your thoughts. If you don't control what you think, you can't control what you do. Simply, self-discipline enables you to think first and act afterward." ~ **Napolean Hill***

To be intentional and take control of your thoughts, you can try these steps if you find yourself headed toward a negative thought cycle:

Tell yourself to stop – give your brain a direct order to cease the negative thought.

Replace it with a positive thought, put a spin on your current thought or change it altogether.

Change direction – distract yourself with an activity such as calling a friend, watching a movie or taking a walk.

Allow the thought to play out in your mind – ask yourself, what's the worst that can happen? Then move forward from there, prepared to accept the worst and come up with a plan of how you would handle that.

Write it down – if you can get a thought on paper, you can get it out of your head.

33 RELAX ON THE HOW AND LEARN TO ALLOW

"Sometimes it's okay just to let go, relax into life, float, and let God carry you trusting that He is the ultimate life raft." ~ Mandy Hale

Earlier, we talked about how letting go is not a free fall because God already has a plan. But too often, we get caught up in the details of God's plans. We want to know HOW God is going to do it, WHEN God is going to do it, WHERE God is going to do it, and WITH WHOM God is going to do it. Most logical-type people are great planners. And as with most planners, you probably believe that the devil is in the details. So you are used to asking WHY, WHAT, WHEN, WHERE and WHAT IF. I am here to remind you to relax. When you let go and you're falling into place, stop riddling your mind with all these questions during your fall into place. Relax. Enjoy the scenery. Enjoy the ride. God is going to reveal to you exactly what you need to know, when you need to know it. Remember, God made you. He created you to be logical and He created you to be a planner. He will give you what you need – which is different from what you want. Allow God to be God. God is the master planner and you are His apprentice. How can you learn from the master if you are always jumping in with your plans or with a million and one questions? Stop. Surrender. Be still. Be quiet. Listen. And take notes.

After my last relationship ended, I spent some time wondering how things were going to work out for me. Although I was only 33 years old at the time, I felt as if I was over my prime and I only had a few good years left. I knew that I didn't want to rush back into a relationship. But, at the same time, I really wanted to know how things were going to work out for me. Deep in my heart and in my spirit, I knew that I was going to be a wife and a mother. But, according to my plans and my outlines, I did not see that happening before I turned 40. Part of me wanted to give up on my dream of being a wife and a mother. But a bigger, deeper part of me said, "No. Don't give up." So I prayed and meditated and asked God HOW was He going to work this out. And do you know His answer? Don't worry about the HOW. It may not happen how YOU think it will happen or when you think it will happen, but just know that it WILL happen.

"We must be willing to let go of the life we have planned, so as to have the life that is waiting for us." ~ Joseph Campbell

The revelation gave me such peace. I am so used to planning every single aspect of my life. I am used to having multiple plans and contingency plans, looking at all possibilities and all possible outcomes. My brain is constantly thinking, planning, moving. So when I was told to simply relax and allow things to happen – yes, I had a small panic attack ... but then I reminded myself that God hasn't failed me yet, why would He fail me now? And there is more than one way to skin a cat. I know that I am going to find true, lasting love. There is no doubt in my mind about that. But I have let go of the notion that I have to give birth to children. In honesty, that wasn't a huge desire of mine. My desire is to be a mother. Being a mother can come in all kinds of forms – birthing children, adopting children, being a godmother, etc. I realized that what is important is that my heart's desire is fulfilled. HOW God chooses to fulfill my heart's desire – I'll let Him handle that. I have enough things going on in my life that I have to plan and coordinate. God has been in the business of turning men into fathers and women into mothers – He has much more experience than I have. So, I'll let the Master handle this.

And that's what I told God. I actually said to God, "God, I'll let You take care of this. I know that You will fulfill my desires. And I trust You to fulfill my desires in the best way. I have other work that You have directed me to do and I will focus my time and my energy on that. I trust You."

Since then, I have not felt anxious about getting married or having children. I haven't felt worried. I haven't felt scared or unsure. When you learn to relax and allow God to do His work, a peace comes over you in a way that you would not have experienced any other way. Peace is much more important than knowing every little detail of God's plan. Knowing every little detail is what keeps you up at night. Relaxing and allowing is what will give you a great night's sleep so you feel refreshed, energized and ready to walk in your purpose.

> "Relax and enjoy life. Know that whatever you need to know is revealed to you in perfect time and space sequence." ~ Louise Hay

As you drive along your journey in life, you'll find that confidence in God's love is always coupled with trust. When love and trust are combined, they are like a match to faith. They will ignite your confidence so that you can ride anywhere that God is taking you without fear.

34 THINK OF GOD AS THE UNIVERSE

"If you really could fit God in a file, you wouldn't need to believe in God, you know, you'd just go get the file like a box of corn flakes off the shelf." ~ Mitch Albom

God is bigger than what you currently think He is. Through our upbringing, teachings and even our own understanding, God has become more human than supernatural.

During my journey to self-discovery and spiritual alignment, I read tons of books, listened to spiritual thought leaders from all across the world, and watched countless videos. My goal was to explore and learn all that I could, and take from it what I thought was good and solid, and apply it to my life. One thing that I noticed is that many of today's spiritual thought leaders now referred to "Universe" instead of "God." Because I still aligned myself with Christianity, anytime I heard the word "Universe," I simply replaced the word with "God." But for some reason, the impact wasn't the same. This really bothered me. How in the world could the concept of God be less effective than the concept of Universe? So I prayed and asked God what was going on in my head. One day, it came to me. The reason that the concept of God was so limited to me is because God was still in a box. In my up-bringing and teaching, I was told what God does and does not do:

God doesn't speak directly to us anymore.

God doesn't get involved in human affairs.

God is only concerned about how everything will serve Him.

God is harsh and mean.

God had been reduced to human form. God had limitations. God was removed and far away. But when I thought about the scientific concept of the universe, the universe was never spoken of in limited terms:

There is no beginning or end to the universe.

The universe is all encompassing.

We are a part of the universe.

The universe responds to what we do as humans.

The universe is everywhere and in everything, and everything is a part of the universe.

The universe doesn't have limitations.

When I talked about God and the universe, the mental image was also different. God had been humanized so much that when I thought of God, I saw a human image in my mind's eye. When I think of the Universe, I don't have a mental image. If I do, it is an image of vastness, stars and no boundaries.

With a humanized, limited view of God, it was impossible for me to truly embrace who God is and what He can do and who I am and what I can do.

"When you give up on your dreams, you put God in a box. After all, you are His creation. He made you for a purpose. Therefore your life cannot be limited any more than God's love can be contained." ~ **Nick Vujicic**

As a math and science geek, math and science make perfect sense to me. But I realized that in order to truly internalize who God is and what He can really do, I had to equate God with the universe and replace my mental image of God with the mental image of the universe.

God = The Universe

God ≠ Human Images

God ≠ Limitations

When I took God out of the box and understood the concept of God as I do the concept of the universe, my world changed. What I expected of myself changed. For the first time, I fully understood and accepted that NOTHING is impossible for God, as the scripture says. Scripture became much more powerful and relevant for me.

Because I have God in me and God is limitless, I believe that I am limitless in what I can do, where I can go and in the influence that I have. This is where God wants us to be. Throw away the box. Burn the man-made images of what man thinks God looks like. See God for who He truly is – limitless. And since you are made in the (spiritual) image of God – you too are limitless when you recognize the power of God that is within you.

The same God who is powerful enough to create worlds cares deeply for you and me. He created the universe to display His might and show us His infinite love. He is so big that He is not bound by time or space, and yet He wants to have a personal relationship with each one of us.

35 EXPECT THE BEST

Miracle (n) – 1) An everyday occurrence for those who realize anything and everything is possible. 2) The norm.

Being the logical thinker that you are, believing in miracles can be a bit of a challenge because you've been taught that miracles do not follow logic and reason. But what if I told you that miracles are logical and reasonable? Throughout this section and this book, you've heard me say time and time again that nothing is impossible for you because nothing is impossible for God. If nothing is impossible for God, isn't it reasonable and logical to expect the unexpected greatness that can come from God? Sometimes, we choose not to believe in miracles because they don't fit into the box of our world. But God is bigger than just you. God is in everything and He created everything. Remember to think of God as the universe. God is just as awesome and expansive as the universe.

Sometimes, we choose not to expect the best or expect miracles because of past disappointments. How do you handle this? How do you continue to expect the best and expect miracles when the thing you've been hoping for and praying for doesn't happen?

You continue to expect the best by believing that the best is happening. There have been times when I've been getting ready for work and I can't find my car keys or my car wouldn't start because I left the inside light on overnight. On one particular occasion I was so angry and frustrated because I had an 8 a.m. meeting and I wasn't going to be on time. Being the Type A personality that I am, I HATE being late. But when I finally got on the road, I realized that I was being protected from a terrible car accident that I may have been involved in had I left on time.

I also remember a time praying for the healing of a loved one. I prayed and cried and prayed and cried. But it didn't happen. The healing never came. It wasn't until maybe a year or so later that I understood why her healing did not come. It was because her ministry was in her medical condition. The life she lived in spite of her condition, the courage and the fearlessness and the hope she displayed was an inspiration to so many people, including myself. The miracle was not in her healing. The miracle was in the lives that she touched.

> *"Miracles occur naturally as expressions of love. The real miracle is the love that inspires them. In this sense everything that comes from love is a miracle." ~ Marianne Williamson*

Choose to believe in miracles. Believe in the seemingly impossible. Again, I know that this is hard for you to wrap your brain around because miracles do not follow logic. But I'm not asking you to believe in HOW miracles will happen. I am asking you to choose to believe that miracles CAN happen and are happening in your life. Take God out of a box. God is much bigger than what you could have ever imagined. Literally, there is nothing impossible with God. Since you have the spirit of God within you, then that means that nothing is impossible for you! Let that sink in for a moment ... Yes. It's okay to do a happy dance. ☺

*"I am realistic – I expect miracles." ~ **Wayne Dyer***

The Bible reassures us that as Christians, miracles will always be a part of our lives. Instead of focusing on what wonders God can do for you today, concentrate on developing your personal relationship with Him. As you follow Him every day, listening to His guidance and will for your life, you will become more like Him … and that is the greatest miracle of all.

REFLECTION

Use the lines below to express your thoughts and insights gained in this section. Describe how you can apply what you've learned in your everyday life.

_____

_____

_____

_____

_____

_____

_____

_____

_____

_____

_____

_____

_____

_____

SECTION VI

CONCLUSION

You have just finished reading Engineering Faith and how to apply different tips to your life. My journey to discovering how to engineer my faith was not an easy journey. At times, it was quite lonely. I want to encourage you to do a few things:

1. Keep this book close by as a quick reference guide when you need to be reminded of how to apply your faith to everyday situations.

2. Build a support system. You do not have to go on this journey alone. Pray and ask God to reveal to you who your support system should be. You should have someone to fill each of these roles.
   a. Spiritual Confidant
   b. Motivator/Encourager
   c. Cheerleader
   d. Accountability Partner
   e. Coach/Counselor (as needed)

3. Never give up. The road to engineering your faith is a life-long journey. You will encounter different terrains along the way. No matter how hard or how easy the road may get, stay focused, stay intentional and remember your lessons on faith. Your treasure and your reward are just over the next hill.

4. Share your story and your experience with others. During my journey, there were times when I felt that no one would understand what I was going through. Share your story with others through casual conversations. By sharing your journey, you will encourage others to share theirs. And you will also encourage someone who is going through what you just went through. You never know how you can be a blessing.

Thank you for allowing me to share my stories and my tips to engineering faith. I hope this book is as much of a blessing to you as it was to me.

Until next time, **Live Fully, Live Fearlessly** and **Live Life on Purpose**!

Made in the USA
Middletown, DE
02 April 2019